GET YOUR KIDS

AHEAD IN

10 MINUTES PER DAY

By RIHANNA MISTRY

HTTPS://WWW.FACEBOOK.COM/GETYOURKIDSAHEAD

HTTPS://TWITTER.COM/RIHANNAMISTRY1

WHY YOU SHOULD BUY THIS BOOK

The PURPOSE of this book is to help busy working parents invest in their children by spending just 10 minutes a day with them. This book will teach parents that taking even 10 minutes out of your day can make a real difference in your child's life. That's right I said 10 minutes per day!

Ever wondered why some kids do better at school, university or even their career? Then this book will reveal some of those SECRETS. It will help you empower your child to achieve that GREATNESS.

This book has 50 TIPS on how to invest in your children. Pick and choose these tips as and when you need, **on top** of the 10 minutes a day principle for maximum effect. You don't need to be a teacher to implement these ideas, just a loving parent who will take some time out of your day and use it to invest in your child. Utilise these tips and watch your child stand above their peers.

This book is AIMED at parents of mainly younger children; however the principles can be applied to a child of any age, whether they are 4 months old or 14 years old.

Read this book if you want your children to get ahead and to be SUCCESSFUL in life, in whatever they choose to be.

MY DREAM

Is to simply inspire children to achieve their greatness.

THIS BOOK IS FOR

All parents who want to do the best for their children: Who want their children to succeed, be happy and stand above their peers.

"Education is the most powerful weapon

we can use to change the world" – Nelson Mandela

THE ROADMAP TO THIS BOOK

PART I

THE GOAL

Our **GOAL** as parents is to provide a loving and supportive environment so that our children/dependants can achieve to their maximum potential and be the great success that they want to be.

We must help our children to find their **PASSION** and their **DETERMINATION** within themselves. This is something that is not easy; it may take a long while and also may change from time to time. However there is something we can do now as parents and that is to just help them with the basics. These basics should give them a head start and the skills they need to help fulfil and realise there passion – whatever it may be.

What are you waiting for? Let's start...

ABOUT ME AND WHERE MY DETERMINATION COMES FROM

I am a parent and an IT graduate from the University of Reading. I am an IT consultant working for one of the top IT consultancies in the world. As you can gather I am neither a child expert nor a teacher. I am married and have 2 beautiful children, Mia aged 8 and Vinnie aged 4. But most of all, **I am a parent who believes education begins at home**.

I just want to point out that I am not a writer, or an author. In fact I prefer to be seen as a business woman with a dream to work for one of the top tech companies in Silicon Valley. (I just thought I would get my elevated speech in there, just in case any top executives are reading this book. Wink wink.) One of my big passions is to share my own parenting experience and views to help other parents. I have used my business knowledge and skills, and applied it to parenting.

As successful as I am in my career, I have written this book because I feel I could have achieved more in my personal and work life:

- If I got better grades.
- If I seized more opportunities.
- If I did more extracurricular activities.
- If I had an opportunity to talk about myself, when I was a child. E.g. What I was doing in school, what I enjoyed, where I was struggling.

- If I was more confident (which all of the above bullet points give you).
- If I had more friends.
- But most of all **if my parents had been able to invest more time in me as a child**.

Nowadays my determination comes from seeing other successful children. I want my children to be part of this group and I want to ensure that they don't miss out on good opportunities. Whether that is an entrance offer to a good university, a good job offer or even having a chance to have like minded friends. This book will reveal the secrets of why these children do better at school.

There are times when I drop my son off at nursery, and I see other children that are not as bright as my son, and "I ain't no tiger mother." When I talk to the teachers they tell me how some of these kids haven't even seen a book before they join nursery. I mean come on, sharing a book with your child is the most basic pastime you can do, surely? Sharing a book is such a beautiful thing. I personally did not realise the full impact of this until one day my son came home from nursery with a mother's day card. Inside the card it read:

I LOVE MY MUMMY because... "we read books together and I love it".

Obviously my son did not write this as a 3 year old, but the teacher had clearly asked my son why he loved his mummy and this was his answer. This sentiment was really touching and made me realise how important reading to your children is, not just for learning purposes, but for good quality time with your children as well. Messages like this really bring home what raising children is all about. This is something we forget in our repetitive and busy lives. My son loves it when I read to him. We talk about the book, the story, the pictures, and anything else that is relevant. Some books we read over and over again, namely Billy goats gruff!

Hearing stories like this is probably the reason why the children's literacy charities have been created. One particular charity called the Book Trust charity give out books for free and leaflets to educate parents about how important it is to read a book. Even my own mother read with me and her English is not that great! So I am really disappointed when parents do not take some time out and read to their children.

It is also disheartening, when I see my daughter's class. She is 8 years old and I see children who are doing maths and English that is aimed at 4 year olds – reception class kids. I'm not talking about the kids who maybe don't have the mental capacity. I'm talking about normal everyday kids, who are bright and bubbly and who clearly have a zest for life. Unfortunately their family life is not ideal and whose parents for whatever reason do not spend the time to make the difference. This not only disappoints me because these children are losing out, but they are also holding my child back. If we want our children to get ahead, we must all work together to succeed together.

I hope you can see that life events have led me to be passionate about making the most of my time with my children. To help them get ahead in school, gain confidence and allow them to achieve amazing successes. The lessons I have learnt as a child and as a parent have enabled me to write this book and show you that even 10 minutes investment per day can make an enormous difference in your children's life.

One of the other key reasons why I have written this book is because other parents regularly ask me: "How do my kids do so well at school?" "How does my daughter pass all her maths targets in one week, when others take months?" "How did she learn to read by the age of 4?" This book will help to answer these questions.

MY MISSION AS A PARENT

So now, I am a parent and I am determined to teach my children as much as I can at home in a fun and in an everyday way. I see it as more of a lifestyle choice rather than a chore.

As far as schools are concerned, I leave them to teach my children all the other subject areas that I am not so good at and also for them to reinforce the principles that I have already taught them.

I also want to encourage my children to do extra activities, sports, crafts and learning new things. I want them to try a variety of activities to give them character, confidence and an opportunity to sample lots of other wonderful clubs. You never know your child might enjoy it and take it up for life.

My job as a parent is to teach my children to live a happy and healthy life, to provide them with opportunities I never had, to be well rounded and to support them to achieve to their full potential.

Education should begin at home.

LET'S JUST GET SOMETHING STRAIGHT...

I just want to make it absolutely clear, that I never force my children, I never push them and in reality we never do anything more than 1 hour a day. In fact they usually get bored after the first 20 minutes. On average I spend about 15 minutes with them five times a week. One particular summer holiday for the whole 6 weeks, we never even touched a book nor did I invest in them, simply because I was too busy with work and they were too busy playing out! It just goes to show that even if you miss some days but you consistently exercise my tips, you can make a big difference. It is so important that you do not to force your children into doing something they don't want to do. No good parent should have a child that resents them when they get older. After all, they get one childhood and it should be a happy one.

I just want to acknowledge that all children are different and they all have a different starting point in life, so for that reason; I want to make it clear that these are MY opinions and MY ways of working. Many of my opinions have been formed through my experience of being a mother, seeing other parents around me and through reading articles about children and education. Some of these points may not work for you and your children. Some tips you may simply disagree with. If it does not work for you or you disagree with some minor points, it's not a big issue. You should drop it and work on the other tips. So please exercise your judgement and use what works for you. I have written this book to share MY ways of working in the hope that at least some of my ideas will help other families.

OK, without further ado let's get started...

GET THE BASICS RIGHT

None of this book is relevant if you don't get the basics right. Studies have linked poor academic performance to factors such as a lack of sleep, poor nutrition, obesity, and a lack of parental support. Those same studies show higher test scores for students who live in homes where healthy habits, regular routines, and where good communication exists.[1] To be fair, if you have bought this book you are most likely providing the basics already. Either way here is a list of my basics: -

Feed your kids well.

This is a no brainer. Ensure your children eat their fruit and vegetables. They should have a varied and nutritious diet. As parents we should set good meal plans for our children and ourselves. There is enough publicity out there on this issue. Remember they say breakfast is the most important meal of the day; especially if you want your children to keep their concentration level up during the day at school, enabling them to do their best. Also it seems so obvious, but you need to keep your children hydrated with lots of water. Studies have shown children who are well hydrated do better in school; hence this is why children are allowed to take water into classrooms with them nowadays.[2] If you want further advice on what to feed your children, there's lot of information on the internet. You can buy books on this subject and if you still not sure, visit your GP who will no doubt give you some advice.

---

[1] According to https://www.healthychildren.org
[2] From http://www.nydailynews.com/life-style/health/drinking-water-linked-higher-test-scores-kids-study-article-1.371530

Ensure your kids get lots of exercise.

Trips to the park, walks around where you live, letting them play out with friends (supervised of course) are all examples of exercise which is free and can be achieved daily. One game I am particularly fond of is tig/tag. We play this game everywhere, in the house, on our way to school and just everywhere. It is guaranteed to get their heart beating. Any sort of sports activity is good. I don't know what it is with exercise, but it somehow clears the brain ready for a fresh start.

Ensure your kids get the right amount of sleep.

Sleep is so important. Having regular routines at bed time also help set a standard. If your child gets the right amount of sleep you will ensure you do not get an irritable child on your hands the next day. A child that is well rested will absorb a lot more information during the day.

Teach your kids good habits.

It is so important we teach our kids good healthy habits. Habits such as: washing their hands before dinner, brushing their teeth, combing their hair, giving them a bath regularly. Where I come from in England, in this day and age, can you believe that kids have rotten teeth before the age of 5? It is hard to believe but it is true, hence this is why I want to mention this point!

As part of teaching children good habits, we should also teach them to be organised. For example, before you go anywhere ask your children what they need to take with them. Packing school bags and lunch bags the night before school makes everyone's life much easier. Another example of being organised is planning and getting children's homework done before it needs to be handed in. It is common sense, however even I have to step back sometimes when things seem to be getting overwhelming and I feel I am rushing about everywhere. Stepping back, prioritising and reorganisation usually helps keep the day running smooth again.

Provide a secure and loving home.

This is things like providing a stable home, providing consistency and good routines. Another example is providing discipline in a uniform manner; this helps support consistency in your child's life. You should be a loving parent, listen to your children and do what you need to, in a fair way to meet their needs.

Provide them space for creativity and play

Playing is a mandatory activity for all children. It helps them be imaginative, creative, get exercise, develop their emotions, build on their personality, have fun and learn new things. It really helps them to develop their thinking and problem solving skills. All these traits are needed for when they become adults. As parents, we should give them lots of time to play and allow them to develop in the most natural way.

MY 50 TIPS

PREFACE TO MY 50 TIPS

Some of my tips you may be doing already, probably in dribs and drabs and you may not even know that you are doing it. Most of these points are common sense, however my tips will help you re-enforce yours ideas, give you confidence in what you are doing and also give you permission to get on with it as more of a plan and a strategy to help your child achieve their full potential.

As a parent you should acknowledge that every child is different and each child will learn in their own time and way. So therefore some tips may work well for some children better than others. It is important that you mix and match tips to ensure variety for your sanity and of your child! In my typical week, I might exercise one tip for a few days and then move onto another tip for a couple of days. I might then take a break for a few days and then exercise two or three tips all in one day. So use it in flexibly for maximum affect.

The first five tips are the most important to me, after that they are in no particular order. However they are still vital and should all be used in equal manner. Everybody has different priorities and ways of working, so take it with a pinch of salt and prioritise these tips as per what you think is most important to you.

1. #EQUALITY FOR ALL

First of all, I believe all children should have an equal right whether they are a boy or girl, race or religion, disabled or not, or any other diversity that they may face. Based on this we should instil good values in ALL of our children and teach them that education is a beautiful thing and they all have an equal right to access it.

Malala Yousafzai once said that school does not only teach us maths, English or any other core subjects. It also teaches us that we are all equal. All, children are required to wear uniform and we all sit together boy or girl. It teaches us to communicate, how to express ourselves and how to work with others. It teaches us discipline, routine and other soft skills.

I passionately follow Malala Yousafzai and Michelle Obama on social media as they both advocate education for girls. This is especially because they often outperform boys at school. With the right support they can achieve great successes. Sadly not everyone agrees with this view and we are robbing the human race of great achievement and progress. I am very lucky in this respect because my father is a great believer in equal rights. He allowed me to further my education as much as I wanted to.   Some Indian parents from the same generation as my father did not give their daughters the same opportunities. So for this I am truly blessed. Thankfully times have changed and all Indian parents I know do focus on education no matter what sex their children are.   He also used to let me watch him fix cars and learn about this trade. He never once said fixing cars is a male thing. He taught me how to drive and he even taught my mum to drive in the early seventies. Now that really was unheard of in the Asian community in England. I really feel that my father was very modern for his generation and for that I am thankful.

One of my friends is completely deaf. She is similar age to me and really inspiring. When I was at university, she managed to get a placement in Australia and she lived there doing her work experience. I mean, that's the other side of the world! When I was job hunting, she spent a few months in the only deaf school in the whole of south India. Out there she helped other deaf children. This school was really primitive and did not own any computers. When she came back to England she organised a big fun raising party to buy some computers for the school. The party was crazy. Once one person starts donating, everybody gets in the donating spirit. Next thing you know the average Jo are donating £10,000 a go. She raised thousands of pounds and she returned to India to help the school buy lots of computers. The computers helped the children gain skills to help with their communication methods. She is a truly amazing person and only because her parents always believed in her and pushed her. Every time she had doubts, they said "YES, you can do anything you want to do and we will help you get there!"

We all have an opportunity in a way to champion - equality for all. We should use our privileged education to champion this further. Every little helps, from being a good role model to volunteering in schools. Wherever your life leads you, if you see an opportunity to champion equality, we should make the effort and do so, especially equality in children.

In Short

Let's give every child, in whatever diversity they face an equal chance.

BEING EQUAL TIME TAKEN: Zero minutes

2. #HOME FIRST

Education begins at home. This is true for every child, no matter who they are or where they come from in the world. Children learn from us as parents every day and in every way. We should be smart, hardworking and positive role models for our children. It is important to make some time at home on top of your daily routine for them. This is to give them some 1-2-1 attention and help them to further their academic and other skills.

Modern lives are far too busy, and if you are like me it just feels like there is no time in the day. So in order to make some time at home, you have to sacrifice something else. I often have to put housework on hold, and I have even skipped being a school governor. So many parents at my child's school have asked me to be a school governor. Although I can probably make some difference in the school, I feel the current school governors are like minded to me and therefore I feel I would not add much value to the school. Instead I prefer to stay at home and make a difference in my child's progress.

While you are at home, I suggest you create a space where you and your children can sit together and learn. A creative environment can make learning so much more enjoyable.

Remember, teachers want parents to send their kids to school with a good work ethic and good behaviour. Even 10 minutes a day with your child can make a real difference. If you have more time, then that is even better.

In Short

Take some time out of your day, forgo what you need to and start educating your child at home first.

CREATE SOME SPACE FOR LEARNING: 10 minutes (one time activity only)

TAKING SOME TIME OUT AT HOME: At least 10 minutes per day.

3. #THE 10 MINUTE PRINCIPLE EXPLAINED

This is one of the key tips in the book. I champion taking 10 minutes out a day at least to invest in each of my children. If you have more time then, that is even better. I say 10 minutes because it is not that much and we should all have that time to spare. If we take 10 minutes a day out daily then already in week you have invested 70 minutes (1 hour 10 minutes). If you decide that weekends are for fun only and you choose to drop the 10 minutes per day, then you can achieve 50 minutes investment per week. That's still quite considerable. I prefer to stick to the 10 minutes a day rule if I can, however that 10 minutes really needs to be focused. There should be no TV in the background, no music and no distractions. That focused 10 minutes is short and sweet and gives you enough time to teach them at least one principle and watch over them while they practise a few questions. When you teach them only one point a day they should actually absorb it. They should also understand it, enjoy it, practise it, and ultimately not get bored of it. Over a week you should be able teach them at least 5 points, and have enough time to practise.

Let me go over a few examples and prove to you that it only takes 10 minutes to teach one point. For example, my daughter gets maths targets which are called passports in her school. Once she achieves those targets she gets another group of maths targets. She is pretty much left alone to learn these passports at home. My view is to spend 10 minutes with her daily and explain each point. By the end of the week she is usually ready to be tested on the passport. My daughter passes her passports weekly or sometimes fortnightly. A lot of her classmates pass their targets 6 monthly. There is a big difference here and one I frankly wonder about.   This could be because the child doesn't understand each target, lacks motivation and mostly it is because the parents don't spare a few minutes to explain it to them.

This is what her typical maths targets look like:

1.   I can count forward and backwards in multiples of 9
2.   I know by heart the multiplication facts for 9 up to 9 X 12
3.   I know by heart all division facts for 9 up to 108
4.   I can recognise and use cube numbers and the notation for cubed

Over the next few pages I give you four examples of my 10 minute a day principle.

Day 1 – Point 1

I can count forward and backwards in multiples of 9

So it is Monday. I sit with my daughter and grab a piece of paper. There is no real theory behind point 1. So I tell her the first 10 numbers in the 9 times table.

09, 18, 27, 36, 45, 54, 63, 72, 81, 90.

Notice after the first number 9, that the tens INcrease by 1 and the units DEcrease by 1. This rule only applies up to the number 90 and after 90 it follows a different path.

The other way of counting up in 9's is just add 10 to the previous number and then take away 1.

Example: $9 + 10 = 19$ then $19 - 1 = 18$.

For counting downwards in 9's, the same theory is applied backwards, Take 10 away and then add 1.

Best thing for you to do now is write a list of numbers on a piece of paper starting with the number 9. See if you can spot any patterns. She should then write a list which looks like my list I wrote her. This would take my daughter less than 5 minutes, if she gets the point first time around. If she doesn't I am still around for her to let her ask questions.

Now how long did it take you to read everything under Day 1? It took me less than 5 minutes to read it slowly and my daughter to get the principle. On top of this I gave her 5 minutes to practise.

Day 1 – Point 1: Achieved in less than 10 minutes. Now I tell Mia to go and play outside.

Day 2 – Point 2

I know by heart the multiplication facts for 9 up to 9 X 12

Today is Tuesday. Let's just have a quick practise of counting in 9's again. So she recites the 9 times tables. I correct any ones that are wrong, and explain the principle again. I also focus on counting in 9's over 90, because that follows a slightly different pattern. This takes me less than 5 minutes.

Now point 2 is similar to point 1. So today I just write the following on a piece of paper:

1 X 9 = 9
2 X 9 = 18
3 X 9 = 27
Etcetera up to
10 X 9 = 90

I then tell her to go away and memorise it and look for any patterns. If you find patterns then it is easier than memorising it. So she spends the rest of the time trying to memorise it.

Day 2 – Point 2: Achieved in 10 minutes. I now tell Mia to go and watch some TV.

Day 3 – Point 3

I know by heart all division facts for 9 up to 108

Today it is Wednesday. Point 3 is similar to point 2 and point 1. So I randomly ask her a few 9 times tables. If she gets a few wrong, I ask her to go back to her sheet and try to memorise it again. I also ask her to count forwards and backwards in 9's. If she gets a few wrong, I ask her to practise some more in her head when she gets a chance.

So today I write on a piece of paper the division facts for her and ask her to look at it and memorise it again. Sometimes there is no easy way of learning the times tables other than memorising it.

$9 \div 9 = 1$
$18 \div 9 = 2$
$27 \div 9 = 3$
Etcetera up to
$90 \div 9 = 10$

She then goes away and learns it.

Day 3 – Point 3: Achieved in less than 10 minutes. I then tell Mia to spend 5 minutes on it and then go and play with her brother.

Day 4 – Point 4

I can recognise and use cube numbers and the notation for cubed

It is now Thursday. This point is super easy. When we say 5 cubed. We mean 5 X 5 X 5 or 3 lots of 5's. Looking at the question it looks like you don't need to work it out. When the teacher asks you what it means, you just tell them it means X times X times X. So what does 7 cubed mean then? Do you get it? Since this was super easy, I will just ask her random 9 times tables and division questions.

Day 4 – Point 4: Achieved in less than 2 minutes. The rest of the time we just revised.

_____

At this rate by the end of the week, it looks like she will get tested. As the content is fresh in her mind she will pass the test. I don't think I need to give you any more examples. I hope I have proved my 10 minutes of focused principle teaching can make a real difference.

JUST TO BE CLEAR

Now you can utilise the rest of the tips in the book on top of the 10 minutes per day principle for maximum effect.

If you struggled to find 10 minutes in the day or you have missed a few days; the rest of the tips should show you how else you can make a difference and teach your child in other ways.   Remember the tips are flexible and can be incorporated into your lifestyle.

In Short

10 minutes of your day on a focused session can really add up and make a big difference to your child's success.

FOCUSED INVESTMENT TIME: 10 minutes per day

4. #GET YOUR PARTNER ON BOARD

If you have a partner then you should involve them in your child's learning path. The first step to getting your partner involved is to talk to them about how you want to help your children to advance in school. Have a conversation on this general subject and share your thoughts.

You can then involve them by sharing what you believe are the goals to help your child progress. If you have the goals stuck on a wall somewhere, then you do not need to communicate the goals to your partner. The idea is that they should see it for themselves.

In my experience it's better to give them responsibility with certain tasks and let them get on with it in their own way. I find that if you interfere with what they are doing, it can just lead to arguments and that just wastes everybody's time. I give my husband tasks like, "it's your job to teach Mia fractions this week" or "can you read with Vinnie this week as I have to catch up with some reading of my own." Whichever way they choose to do their task, the outcome should hopefully be the same.

You can involve them by just having a 5 minute conversation with them daily. I often find myself saying things like: "Mia read well today, however she needs to look up new words that she did not understand in the dictionary, so make sure she does that". Or: "Vinnie needs to focus on writing the alphabet as he gets his B's and D's mixed up." Throwing the one liners out there, makes everyone effectively sing from the same hymn sheet and hopefully reminds your partner that if he/she has some downtime, then they know what to focus on.

If your circumstances are different and you don't have a partner for whatever reason, do not worry, the rest of the tips in this book should give you good stead. If your partner doesn't live with you but you have a good amicable relationship with them, then it is worth having a conversation with them to explain what you want to achieve. In the hope you can work together to achieve your common goals.

The ideal scenario is that your partner takes an active role with your child. As they are doing this they will notice which areas your child is good at and what they are struggling with. Then they should also be throwing one liners back at you. So the ideal scenario is that the teamwork will make the dream work!

In Short

Involve your partner. Share your children's goals with them.

CONVERSATION TIME: 5 minutes per day

5. #LET'S READ BOOKS

Books are great teaching aids. They teach adults and children a tremendous amount and not just how to read. They teach us empathy, morals and vocabulary; they build on our thought processes, teach us about the whole big wide world and how diverse it is and that's just to name a few.

Reading together should start from a young age. I started when my kids were 4 months old. Take some time out before bedtime and do this. You will find it will help provide a calming environment and also adds routine to your bedtimes. I read to my son most nights. One book may take me 10 minutes to read and I spend another 10 minutes after that to talk about what we have read (that is if he hasn't fallen asleep already). Even my daughter's school champions reading for 10 minutes per day.

Books are everywhere nowadays. I have lots of children's books on my bookshelf at home. On the last count, about 100 of them were free. Some I got from my health visitor via the book trust charity. Some I got free from my local children's centre. Once I went to a car boot sale and bought a job lot of what I would only class as new modern children books for £10. What a bargain! You can even buy cheap books from charity shops or auction websites. If you really don't want to spend any money, then even the old school method of borrowing from a library works too. You can even ask other mothers if they have a few books they want to get rid of or if they will kindly let you borrow some. Books are everywhere, so there should be no excuse for not reading with your children.

When they get older and as they become independent readers, you will not have to read to them. However it is still important that you check in with them, and ask them what they are reading. Here is a sample of questions you can ask them.

- What is the book about?
- What have you learnt?
- What do you think will happen next?
- Do you like the book?
- What are your best and worst parts?

Check that your child understands the book. Once a child learns to read, the next level is about understanding what they read and their interpretation of the text. I believe it helps form ideas and develop thoughts. If they are not getting it, maybe it's time to step in and read with them chapter by chapter, pausing at regular intervals to check their understanding. I always ask my daughter to summarise what happens, because that is just a skill on its own! If they don't understand what is happening then we should summarise for them!

I also suggest that they write new words that they don't know on a piece of paper. This is then something they can look up later to build their vocabulary.

One thing I have learnt is my daughter does not like fiction books. She is like me and prefers to read biographies and fact books. So if you find your child doesn't like reading, then here are a few suggestions on how you can change that pattern.

- Find other categories of books, fiction, nonfiction, stories, biographies, fact books etc. Let your child choose.
- Read with them aloud and add some passion.
- Watch the film, if one has been made. There are lots of popular kid's books that have been made into films. Roald Dahl's - Matilda, BFG and others. David Walliam's – Gangsta Granny, Millionaire Boy and others. JK Rowling's - Harry Potter series.
- Take a break. Even I need a break from reading time to time.

Whatever your children prefer to read, make sure they understand it. As a family you should adopt reading into your lifestyle and hopefully you can all learn new things together.

In Short

Reading is a beautiful thing.

READ A BOOK: 10 minutes per day.

TALK ABOUT A BOOK: 10 minutes per day.

6. #START TEACHING THEM FROM YOUNG

You should start teaching your child from the earliest opportunity. I started teaching my children from 4 months officially. The younger they are, the more they will absorb. Education is a lifelong experience and while we are still around, I am afraid it is up to us as parents to help them.

As they get older, they will get more independent and thus they will need less and less of our time. However don't get complacent as there may come a time when you need to step in and start guiding them again.

Did you know, Finnish children do better at school and university, compared to their European counterparts and they don't even start school until the age of 7? There are many factors to their success, however it could be because the child gets 1-2-1 attention up to the age of 7 and this is when they absorb the most.

In Short

It is never too early to start teaching your children.

START TEACHING YOUNG: As part of your 10 minutes per day

7. #YOUR BABY CAN READ

Would you believe me when I said that, when my daughter was one years old she could read about 50 basic words?

Let me tell you how this came about. When I was pregnant I saw a programme called Richard and Judy, in which an American professor Dr Bob Titzer came in and talked about how his 1 year old daughter could read about 50 or so words. I was truly amazed and did not believe it until I saw the clips. After my daughter was born I did some serious contemplation and I finally decided I would try his techniques on my daughter.

His technique basically involves showing words to children on a daily basis until your child recognises the word. They are like flash word cards. Initially I was worried this was a con or could impact the development of my child. My view was to just give it a go and review regularly.

I tried to source his DVD's in England with no luck, in the end I had to ship them in from America. It cost me over £80 for the full set, so it was a significant investment. His advice was to use the DVD's daily, but I used his approach intermittingly and it worked. By the time she was one she could read about 50 simple words. By the time she was 3 years old she could read all the "first reader" children's books. Soon after we started on children's chapter books at the age of 5. Most of her friends at this age were only just starting to learn to read. As she already knew how to read, this gives us more time to teach her other things like advancing her maths and other subjects. All I know is that she is definitely top of her class and the school recognises this. Her nursery and her reception teacher were all truly amazed. To help Mia develop her reading further, her class teacher sends her to senior classes to learn higher level English.

It only took me 2 minutes to put the DVD on for her. She really enjoyed them as they sang nursery rhymes and showed pictures in them. She would even ask me to put them on regularly for her.   Unfortunately the DVDS did not work second time round for my son. He just couldn't sit long enough to watch them despite me trying several times. But for my daughter it was a good investment. The DVD's are called "Your baby can read," if you want to look it up.

So my theory behind this secret is that even as adults when we are reading, we actually are not reading. We are recalling words and shapes from our memory to work out what it says on paper.   Try reading this word, can you really read it? Otorhinolaryngologist. Look it up on an internet dictionary site for the actual pronunciation. It is the area of medicine that deals with conditions of the ear, nose, and throat. Ok maybe that was too long and hard; let's try something a bit smaller and more realistic. Try ANEMONE Pronunciation: Uh-nem-uh-nee. Apparently it is a wild flower species. When you read it, did you question if you pronounced it correctly? This proves my theory (however I do appreciate that children learn to read in their own different ways).

If you can't get a hold of the DVD's or you think they are expensive then there are other videos that are similar that come on the children's channels and even YouTube has similar videos with similar concepts.

In Short

Start your children young and give them a head start because your baby really can read with Dr Bob Titzer's methods.

PUT A DVD OR VIDEO ON: Less than 2 minutes per day

8. #FLASHCARDS ARE GREAT

Flash cards hold the same principles as watching a video and can be great learning aids. They can be shown to a child at regular intervals, so that the child can recall the information. For example, if you write some words on a card, then flash these cards at your preschool children and read out what is written; they should start recognising the words. I remember my primary school teacher doing this. It is not just words you can use it for; you can do colours and objects or anything else, whatever your imagination takes you. You can even buy lots of word flash cards at toy shops nowadays, if you want to save yourself the hassle of creating them yourself. My only issue with the cards is that they are more like paper than card, and younger children tend to bend them. So if you are a manufacturer of these cards and you are reading this book – maybe it is time you actually print on tougher cards to make it more robust for younger children.

I would flash these cards and test my children's understanding for as long as they can keep the attention. 10 minutes is a good time to do this. You don't want to overload them or equally bore them. You do this periodically until they learn the points. Simple word cards, examples below. It really is that easy.

Cat	Dog	Log

Once they get older, the flash cards are good for remembering subject specifics for exams. Some of my friends used to really animate their own flash cards. Example of a few flash cards below:

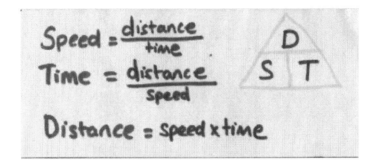

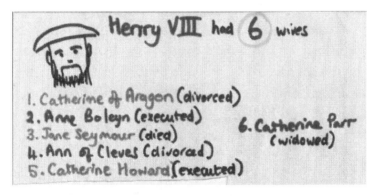

Keep them relatively simple with only a few points per card and add some colour for maximum effect.

In Short

Buy or make your own flash cards and then flash them to your children. Do it at regular intervals until they learn the points.

MAKE SOME WORD FLASHCARDS: 2 minutes for 1 A4 sheet and 10 words

CHILD MAKES SOME SUBJECT AREA FLASHCARDS: 5 minutes, as the child makes each card they will re- member it, and it can be useful for revision later

FLASH SOME CARDS: 10 minutes

9. #LEARNING IS ALL AROUND US

In reality, we all learn new things every day. This is part of human nature. Life is a learning curve and even as adults we are learning new things all the time. The truth is, the more we learn, the more we should realise that there is a lot more to learn out there.

Learning is not an activity you can only do at home or school, it can come in many forms. The best is practical learning, or learning through actions. So we should be able to find 10 minutes per day in some shape or form, whether it is walking to school or talking while you are making the family meal. Sports and activity classes are also learning opportunities. Below are examples how I incorporate learning in everyday activities.

- Practising timetables on my way to school.
- Asking my 4 year old to read door numbers when we are on our walks to the park.
- Maths questions in the car.
- I let them ask me random questions at the dinner table.
- While they are bathing in the bathroom, I have those bath crayons and I use the crayons to write simple words in the bath and I ask my 4 year old what it says. I also do simple arithmetic in the bath with my son. Like what is "4+6?" They also draw in the bath.
- While I am cooking I will ask silly questions, like if there were 10 elephants in the room and 1 elephant walked off. How many tigers are left? Yes I said tigers. This is a trick question, and one my kids have never fallen for. ☺

- While I brush their teeth, I sing nursery songs. Nursery songs are apparently great for building memory in young kids.
- While we are shopping.

Weekends are great for learning too. Wherever you choose to go, shopping, parks, museums, etc. There is always a lot to talk about. You can talk about nature, animals, people, history, food, what products are good and how it is made. The list goes on. Look around and be mindful of the world around us. There are countless opportunities to talk and learn.

Whatever your routine is and whatever your day looks like, you can teach your children in some shape or form.

"Once children learn how to learn, nothing is going to narrow their mind. The essence of teaching is to make learning contagious, to have one idea spark another." – Marva Collins

In Short

Whatever you are doing, look around and be mindful. Talk to your children about the world around you because learning really is all around us.

LEARNING IS ALL AROUND US: Every minute of every day

10. #BE POSTIVE AND HAPPY

It is so important that we are good role models for our children. I think we as parents don't realise how much our children look up to us and as part of that we should be happy and positive people. For those of us that find ourselves repeating ourselves all the time, we should just stop it. Nagging is not a word I like. We all fall in this trap sometimes when daily tasks are just not getting done.

Positive behaviour is a choice we can all adopt. Happy people breed more positivity and believe it or not, it really is contagious. If we are cheerful and positive about teaching our children, then they will also be happy to learn it. Positivity is not just about what language we use, but also about our body language. When we talk about a subject we should talk with passion and joy and really see the excitement in it. I always seem to get excited when my kids get an answer right. A high five is always waiting for them and I even tell my husband when he gets home. He also puts on a smile and gets excited when I tell him. The kids just love it.

Below are a few examples of happy and positive body language we can use. Smiley faces, smiley eyes, high fives, thumbs up, shoulders back to show confidence, jumping in the air, skipping, open and welcoming arms, big hugs. That's just to name a few.

Here are a few positive happy buzz words that we can adopt in our language: great, excellent, fantastic, that's right, outstanding, brilliant, superb, and tremendous.

You can even be positive when they have not done so well. Positive constructive criticism will take them much further than negative language. There is so many ways of turning criticism into a positive action. It is better to tell them what they need to do to fix their work, rather than to put them down and knock their confidence with negative language.

Let me tell you an analogy that I have heard a few times: Imagine a white elephant and a red elephant in the room with you. Now I want you to NOT think about the red elephant. What is in your head? ....

It's the red elephant isn't it? We are all human and when somebody tells us NOT to do something, I don't know about you but I am always curious to know why. Before you know it, the red elephant is all I can think about. Whereas if I told you to focus just on the white elephant. The white elephant is probably what you are thinking about. So it is better to structure your sentences to focus on what needs to be done, rather than what you should NOT have done. This is similar to the cup analogy. How would you describe a cup that is filled with water half way? Would you describe it as half full or half empty? If you described it as half full, then you are probably one of the positive ones. Positive language is the key.

Speaking of red and white elephants, my husband always says: "If you want something doing either,

1. Do it yourself
2. Pay somebody to do it
3. **OR ask your children NOT to do it!"**

(He has obviously got that from somewhere.)

Below are some examples of good and bad language. Take note of the differences and how would you like to be treated. It sometimes takes a while to change your language especially if it is a habit. If it is, then pause for a moment and change.

Situation: Your child has got many questions wrong.

Bad use of language: You have done a bad job. This is terrible. Go do this again

Good Use of language: Umm, you seem to have a few wrong here, but not to worry, I think we need to practise more. Shall we go through a few together?

Situation: Your child's homework is messy and unclear.

Bad use of language: This is really bad, I can't read this. This is not acceptable.

Good Use of language: Wow there is a lot of writing on here. Did you really do this is in your best handwriting? Let's start again, and have clear sections, space things out and do it in our best writing. I will help if you would like?

Situation: You child comes home with bad exam results

Bad use of language: You're pathetic. This is really bad. What are you playing at? Do you want to waste another year at school etcetera?

Good Use of language: Aww, that is disappointing. But let's turn this around, focus on your weak points, practise some more and then next time you won't be in this situation. I will help you if required.

As you can see there is a difference in the negative and positive language. We all make mistakes and there is nothing worse than somebody standing over you and saying "I told you so" or people making a mountain out of a molehill. .

Positive language as you can see, can be more effective and also promote your child's self esteem. As parents, if we are positive and provide constructive advice and then children are also likely to change their attitude. They will find solutions to the problem and not focus on what has happened. If you constantly use negative language, you will probably find that your children will be too scared to approach you for anything. Nobody wants to live in that fear and neither is this productive. Asking how you can help using open ended questions is also a good trait, for example "would you like to clean your room, so you can invite your friends round later?" Rather than using direct language such as "Go clean your room." It's good to point out the benefits of doing something as well, such as "if you get your homework done now, we can go to the park later." So let's change our language and be really positive.

"We must become the change that we want to see."

- Mahatma Gandhi

In Short

Change our attitudes and be positive and happy; In mind and in spirit.

BE POSTIVE AND HAPPY: Minimum effort

11. #GET YOUR CHILD INTO A GOOD SCHOOL

In England, every school is graded by the government. They are graded by the overall effectiveness of the school in the following areas. [3]

- Achievement of pupils
- Quality of teaching
- Behaviour and safety of pupils
- Leadership and management

There are 4 grades you can get:

Grade 1 Outstanding
An outstanding school is highly effective in delivering outcomes that provide exceptionally well for all its pupils' needs. This ensures that pupils are very well equipped for the next stage of their education, training or employment.

Grade 2 Good
A good school is effective in delivering outcomes that provide well for all its pupils' needs. Pupils are well prepared for the next stage of their education, training or employment.

Grade 3 Requires improvement
A school that requires improvement is not yet a good school, but it is not inadequate. This school will receive a full inspection within 24 months from the date of this inspection.

Grade 4 Inadequate

---

[3] Attained from http://www.clerktogovernors.co.uk/what-ofsted-judgements-mean/ website

A school that has serious weaknesses is inadequate overall and requires significant improvement but leadership and management are judged to be Grade 3 or better. This school will receive regular monitoring by Government inspectors.

―――――――――――――――

I am sure other countries in the world also have similar rankings systems. We should use these resources to choose the right school for your children.

Ideally you want your child to go to a school, where they have received a Grade 1: Outstanding or equivalent. This is a no brainer. Good schools can really add value to your child's life and development and can make your life a bit easier too. If all the children in an outstanding school are doing well, then your child should move up with them at a good pace. You should surround your children with a good set of friends and that should push them to achieve more.

In my experience there are very few of these outstanding schools and there is too much competition to get your children in there, especially in my area. In my locality there must be about 7 primary schools in a 10 minute commutable distance, and only 1 school is rated outstanding. This school is a Catholic school, and as a British Indian my children's chances of getting in are seriously slim. So if you can't get your children into the best school around, aim for the second best, Grade2: Good category. Bear in mind that schools in England usually get tested every couple of years and their grading does change. The best schools are ones which consistently stay at outstanding or good. I would be concerned if your child goes to a Grade 3 or Grade 4 school, and I would consider moving.

As a parent I understand that choosing a school is a personal choice and for each of us different factors need to be considered. For example, if you don't have a car then the school needs to be local; if all your child's good friends go to one school, then you may also want your child to go to that school. You might want to choose a school that is near your work, so you can easily drop them off. There are many factors to consider when you choose a school. Whatever it is don't fret if the school is not outstanding. It is worthwhile trying to work out what the schools weakness is. Hopefully all the strategies you employ as a parent will compensate for them and just because your child does not go to the best school, it does not mean they will not achieve their greatness.

If you have the money, then you will most likely send your child to a private school. This should give your child a good head start, especially since the teaching resources should be better and there is a better pupil to teacher ratio. I read in a recent article that state school children do better at university compared to private school pupils[4]. They believe that state school pupils do better because they can cope with being plunged into university with its big student population and diversity, unlike private school pupils who have had a privileged life thus so far. You should take this how you like; I just wanted to share this piece of knowledge with you.

My children go to a good school. The best thing about it is that it is 5 minutes walk away with the most amazing views of

---

[4]Information from
http://www.independent.co.uk/news/education/education-news/state-school-students-get-better-degrees-than-private-school-pupils-with-same-a-levels-10504225.html

farmland on the way. There are times where I feel my child would do better, if the school changed some of its policies. In that instance I just tell the teachers and most good teachers will consider your view and make the change if possible. The world is a changing place and we must all adapt and change as well. This also applies to schools as well. If you have some feedback for the school, then just let them know what it is and give them a chance to improve. If you send your child to a mediocre school, but it's local don't worry. Just think of all the time you have saved in commuting and travel expenses. Use the extra time you have to make up for the schools weaknesses.

In Short

Give your child the best start in life and send them to a good school.

CHOOSE A GOOD SCHOOL: Mandatory

12. #ACTIVITY BOOKS ARE GREAT

Activity books are great, especially if you are like me and wonder what shall I teach them next? They are often written by teachers and cover school curriculums. They also move on to the next logical area in the subject in a strategic manner. Before you buy an activity book make sure you flick through the book and ensure that it is at the right level for your children and the questions will challenge your kids. I say this because for example with my son who is 4 years old, there is no point me buying him a preschool book as he already knows his alphabet and basic numbers. I would be better buying him an age 5+ books. I have the same issue with my daughter, where an age 8/year 3 maths books would be too easy for her. An age 11/year 6 maths book is definitely more appropriate for her. Check out your local book store to see which activity books to buy.

Some activity books may not have enough questions to practise, especially when they are getting the questions wrong. In that case I supplement the book by writing a few questions myself or printing out worksheets from the internet. It is important to stay on the subject until your child gets it, rather than rushing on to something else. If you have spent too long in one area and there is frustration all round, in this instance I would move on and come back to that subject a few weeks or even months down the line (if possible). However make sure you make a note of it as you and the child will probably forget.

Ideally as a parent, you need to spend a minute or two reading the first few lines in each page of the activity book with your child. You should explain what the principle or method is and then just let your child get on with it. Younger kids will need more hand holding.

If you can't afford to buy activity books, then there are some great internet sites where you can download worksheets. On the good sites the worksheets will be in order of difficulty which should help you work out which sheets to print. If you are really creative, then you can make your own worksheets.

Fun activity books can also be great fun and you can learn things. Things like colouring in will help your child with their pencil control. Mazes and spot the difference all really do help in your child's brain development as well. These are great to take on a plane or on journey to help entertain your children.

In Short

Buy some activity books which are at the right level and set your child on them.

BUY AN ACTIVITY BOOK: Whilst out shopping

WALK THROUGH THE METHOD WITH YOUR CHILD: 2 minutes

LET YOUR CHILD WORK ON THE ACTIVITY BOOK: 10 minutes at a time

13. #DON'T FALL FOR THE EDUCATIONAL TOYS GIMMICK

Let's just clarify what I mean by educational toys first. There are lots of educational toys out there. I'm not really talking about baby toys, like rattles or where you press a button and something pops out. Those toys are good for developing baby's motor skills. I am talking about other specific toys aimed more at preschool children (I won't mention any names), like children's laptops.

There is one toy that my niece had which I was never really keen on. You put an electronic pen over words from a ridiculously expensive book and it recognises the word for you and reads it out loud. I am not convinced its value for money but most of all it never really taught my niece how to read. All it did was give the parent back some time in their diary. It wasn't long before my niece completed reading the book and asked for another one. After a buying a few more books at around £5 per book, the parents thought that this was burning a big hole in their wallet and gave up on this technological aid. It really was not providing much value and most of all she did not learn to read from it.

The primary focus for toy manufacturers is to earn money, whether the toy is educational or not. These toys cannot teach your child in its own individual way to provide maximum effect. Don't get me wrong, they may learn something, but maybe not as much as you would like.

My son had one of these children's computer laptops that ask you basic maths questions like, "What is 2+2?" or "What does apple begin with?" The screen is black and white and it is not as appealing as the colour computer tablets. Either way, the laptop is limited in its functionality, he doesn't spend much time on it and he definitely doesn't learn much from it. In my opinion it is a waste of time and money. He learns what apple begins in 2 minutes when I teach him as opposed to really never, even though he has been asked by the laptop many times. This is probably because as a human, I can talk through the sounds and explain why apple begins with A.

It is up to you, whether you want to buy these toys, but from mine and shared experiences from other parents, some of these toys really are a waste of time if you genuinely want to teach your child something. If you want to buy this, to entertain your child then that is a different story.

In Short

Save your money and don't buy these educational toy gimmicks.

TIME SAVED: 1 HOUR OF PURCHASING

14. #ACADEMIC SUCCESS IS NOT EVERYTHING

It is important that we help create well rounded children. To achieve that we need to ensure our children take on a variety of activities, such as swimming, dancing, gymnastics, play dates, playing out, football, tennis, badminton, other sports, cooking, skiing, drawing, writing, languages, crafts, music. The list goes on. Who knows, in these classes they might find their passion.

My view is that we should let them try anything they want to, within reason and within your budget. There will be some activities they try and they get bored of, and others they actually enjoy. The key to this one is letting them experience enough of them before they make their own judgement. Sometimes we may be a little too quick to quit. You will often find children will like the class more if they make a good set of friends in there. Extracurricular activities give your child confidence and character. They also allow your child to make new friends and that is a key skill for life. I find these people to be well rounded, more willing to try out new activities and are generally happier and confident.

I find people who have variety in their life, have the character to blow their own horns more and go the furthest. On the other hand, I know people with first class honours degrees with true academic abilities, who want to get further in their career, but they lack the personality to earn top paying jobs. Ten to fifteen years into their career they are still in an entry level basic job.

In one of my own personal experiences, I went for an interview for a top IT company for my sandwich year, when I was at university. When I got there it felt like half my university classmates were also in there waiting to be called in for an interview. I looked around and I thought to myself, no way am I going to get this job! There were guys in there that had better IT grades than me, and were more tech savvy. In reality they were real IT geeks. If I had to do an IT exam I could never beat these students. In fact I was surprised I even got an interview because I had sent my CV to the company, a day after the deadline. It was just not meant to be but as I was already there, all I could do was my best.

During the interview, I don't know how but the conversation came on to recent holidays. As I had just been to Florida over the Easter break, I talked with such enthusiasm about how great it was. The conversation flowed and I don't even think we talked about IT much. Anyway 2 weeks later I was surprised when I got a call offering me the job, which I happily accepted. This was not an opportunity I was going to pass; after all it was with a global company, in a cosmopolitan city. After I settled in I asked the hiring manager, why they offered the job to me considering there were twenty other IT guys in the waiting room who were well - a lot more technical than I was. His answer was simple. He said, "You were the only one who had character and talked in there." Could you believe it? So the moral of the story is that character can also help you achieve your ambition.

I appreciate we all have busy lives and can't always take our children to clubs and activities. Do you know of anybody else who is trustworthy that can help? I have noticed families who utilise aunts/uncles/godparents/friends. I know one aunt who takes her niece to dance classes every week, so that the parents get time to get on with other tasks. Informal arrangements like this are great. It means mums and dads get time to get on with their house work, while the kids go to a club, and an aunt/uncle gets to spend quality time with their niece/nephew. Everyone is a winner all round.

Just a note about swimming from my experience: Don't expect the school to teach your child swimming. The reality is that they probably only do it for a couple of terms in their whole school life, and they don't learn much. Just think about it, 1 swimming teacher and 30 kids? So many kids in my generation only had a taster lesson at school. Its better they go to separate lessons. It is also a good idea to get them started at the age of 4 even if you have to go in with them. It's actually great fun and lovely quality time.

I recently read that poorer children who do extracurricular activities do better in life, compared to children of a similar background.[5] I would agree with this. I find kids who are challenged make the most of their down time. I heard my daughter say last week: "I have so many clubs going and I am so busy, so I am just going to get my homework done today in my free time."

Some children are not academically gifted; in that case, you need to make them as practical as possible in the hope that they find their success in other professional jobs.

There are many successful people who academically did not do well nor had no interest in school. Entrepreneurs like Alan Sugar, who quit school at 16 to work briefly for the civil service. Shortly after, he then went onto buy a van with his

---

[5] http://www.theguardian.com/education/2016/apr/20/after-school-clubs-can-improve-poorer-childrens-education

savings and sold car aerials and other electronic goods from the back of it. His famous motto is "buy cheap, sell for more." In 1968 he founded the company AMSTRAD, the name was formed out of his initials (AMS) and TRADing. The company began as a general importer/exporter and wholesaler, but soon specialised in consumer electronics. Though his determination and no nonsense attitude, it led to various successes and now he is a business icon, media personality and a political advisor. He is worth billions.[6] Not bad for someone who quit school at 16 huh?

Richard Branson was 15, when he too dropped out of school. He was actually dyslexic. He is currently a business magnate, investor, and philanthropist. He is best known as the founder of Virgin Group, which comprises more than 400 companies. At the time of writing this book, he is worth $4.8 billion. Other successful people who dropped out of school include Aretha Franklin and Quentin Tarantino. Both dropped out at 15. So as you can see from my examples, some people do not make it in school, but can go on to be successful.

When you believe a child is trying their hardest and is not succeeding as much as you like, you should just help them as much as possible and not be a perfectionist. Success may come in small steps for them. One day they will find something that they enjoy and hopefully they can make a living out of it.

---

[6] Information from
https://en.wikipedia.org/wiki/Alan_Sugar#Early_life

In Short

So my point is academic success isn't everything, confidence and character can take you a long way.

OUT OF SCHOOL ACTIVITIES: At least 1 hour a week.

15. #AIM HIGH

We should set high goals for our children. My goal with my kids is that they get into a good grammar school and then onto a great university, preferably from the Russell group. (The Russell Group is a self-selected association of twenty-four public research universities situated in the United Kingdom. The group is widely perceived as representing the best universities in the country.)[7] The better grades they get or the more skills that they acquire, the more choices in life they will have. So if I can help my child get good grades and obtain as many skills as possible, then he/she will have more choices. Choices like which university they want to go to or which career path they take.

Aiming high is not just a long term mission; it can also be a daily challenge as well. Daily examples for your child could be: Doing better homework, reading higher level books compared to their peers, trying to score more goals at a football match or being chosen for a school talent competition. There are lots of targets where you can aim high at. It is important for you to work with your child and decide what the priorities should be. Aiming high will keep your child challenged and give them a strong and inquisitive mind.

So many successful people state that you should aim high, dream big and you can achieve what you want in life with enough determination. This statement should also apply to our children. If your child achieves these goals then that is

---

[7] Definition from https://en.wikipedia.org/wiki/Russell_Group

super fantastic. However if they don't quite get there, then it's not a big issue. Our children should not get downhearted and they should learn the lessons for next time. The child will be wiser and stronger. Remember every failure, will be their pillar to success.

In Short

Dream big, aim high and they shall eventually succeed.

AIM HIGH: Every Day

16.#SET SOME GOALS

In order to #aimhigh, have some goals that your children need to or want to achieve. This can really help in giving you and your child a direction. It doesn't have to be war and peace. I start with the yearly goals.

When my children were younger it was simple goals like:

1. Get them out of nappies
2. Get them off the bottles
3. Teach them to count to 10.

Now that they are older I have yearly goals like:

1. Go ice skating at least once
2. Start dance lessons
3. Get Mia to practice 11 + papers
4. Get Mia to read more.
5. Need to practise those fractions again.
6. Go on holiday
7. Get Vinnie to count to 100.
8. Get Vinnie into football lessons

Notice it is not all just about academic studies; they also include other activities which will all help build a rounded child. Remember that your child's goals should be tailored to them only, depending on what they are good at already and what they need to work on. I would also suggest that you don't have too many goals, as it can seem overwhelming for some parents. Keep them short and simple. Tick them off as you go and if your child completes most of them ahead of your goal setting period, then just go ahead and write some more for them. If your child is older, involve them in the process and then you can both agree on what tasks they need to do, to achieve those targets.

You can set quarterly goals, weekly and even daily goals. I personally don't do weekly and daily goals because for me, that is getting too pedantic, especially when you are a working mother. I just stick to the yearly and 3 monthly goals. My weekly and daily goals are my to do lists, which are personal tasks that I need to do. It may have a few items for the kids, like pay for their swim lessons for example, but rarely does it have goals that further my children. Depending on your personality and time, you should set goals depending on what level your child is, and what they need to achieve next. Remember to #AIM HIGH and ensure that they are challenging. For those parents who are super competitive, it can be a good idea to set goals that are really high. For your children, it may not be easily attainable, but they sure will try and at the end of the goal period, they may nearly get there.

In business, we use an acronym called SMART. It is useful when setting career goals, and can also be used for children and their goals. The meaning is:

S - Specific, significant, stretching

M - Measurable, meaningful, motivational

A - Agreed upon, attainable, achievable, acceptable, action oriented

R - Realistic, relevant, reasonable, rewarding, results-oriented

T - Time-based, time-bound, timely, tangible, track-able

SMART is a really good tool when setting goals and it can give you and your child something to think about.

You should also try the goals and stick it on the notice board. Somewhere where you, your partner and your child can see it, and where you are reminded of what those goals are. Otherwise you may forget and also sometimes you may lose the motivation to achieve those goals. This tip gives you some organisation skills.

In Short

Set some goals and stick it on the wall, remember #AIM HIGH.

SET GOALS: 5 Minutes quarterly

17. #PRIORTISE THOSE GOALS

If as a parent, you are really determined to get your child ahead, you need to prioritise your children's goals. Give each goal a number, where 1 is the highest priority. Some goals may have joint priority. If some of those targets need to be met by a certain deadline, then you and your child need to draw up a schedule to meet that goal. If the goal is big, then break down the goal into smaller more manageable pieces, and work with your child to practise each point a day (if possible). If your child is taking an exam, you need to prioritise learning the area that will give them the most marks or if your child is good at most of the areas, then you need to prioritise your child's weak areas.

Remember priorities change from time to time, so you will need to come back and review regularly, which brings us to the next tip.

This tip is for the more strategic parent.

In Short

Work with your child to prioritise your children's goals.

PRIORTISE THOSE GOALS: 2 Minutes quarterly

18. #REVIEW THOSE GOALS

Once you have set the goals for your children, every so often you should review these goals. I tend to review my children's goals every 3 months or so, to tick off the ones they have achieved and even set new ones. I sometimes find that I change goals because it may become less priority and hence it gets pushed back another year or so. Or I may remove it off the list all together. There are times when my children don't meet the targets, maybe because they just don't get something or we have not had much time to focus on it. If this is the case, I don't beat myself up on it because I need to keep the wheel turning and keep my children learning. We are all humans, and that's life.

Don't forget to #AIM HIGH again, and keep those targets stuck on the wall for a useful reminder!

In Short

Review those goals. Tick off, amend, delete and add to your child list of targets.

REVIEW THOSE GOALS AND SET SOME NEW TARGETS: 5 Minutes quarterly

19. #SKIP OVER THE EASY BITS

This is something I tell my children to do quite regularly, especially in the workbooks. They are only allowed to do this, if I agree that a section is too easy for them. I will ask them once: If they know it and seem confident in that area, then the best plan of action is to skip over it. This is not something you would automatically think to do; however I let them do it to save myself and my children some time. In my mind, this is not adding much value.

There was one particular time, when I asked the teacher to increase the level on an online maths resource that they use. It was too easy for her and hence I wanted to skip over it; to utilise my child time more efficiently and to ensure that she did not get seriously bored. The teacher regularly said no because the resource should be increasing in difficulty automatically on its own. My argument was that she was getting 100% answers right on the 1st go. She had passed maths targets that were 3 years above her age. If that was genuinely the case, that the resource moves up dependent upon my child's ability then my argument was that it was simply not moving fast enough. After some persistence, the teacher agreed to move to the next level, to ensure the maths questions were more challenging and appropriate for her level.

In Short

Skip over the easy bits and ensure you are working on the right level!

TIME SAVED: Considerable

20. #IT'S TIME FOR SOME REVISION

From time to time, you have to remind your children to go back to a subject that they did a while ago. This ensures that principles are really remembered and helps keep those thoughts fresh. I tend to remind my children of the areas that they found difficult. For example, every so often I ask my child to do some multiplication or division. Revision is more applicable as they get older and during exam time. So during exam time, take some time out and help your child revise their subjects whatever it may be. It is worth asking your children to do a mind map of chapters in their learning books after they read it so it is easier to revise.

There was one time where I spent ages trying to get my son to learn the alphabet. To be honest once he knew it I just moved on, because I personally was just bored of the subject. However 2 months on he had forgotten most of the letters. This was so annoying and frustrating. So I had to start again. Whereas if I had taken some time to revise maybe every couple of weeks or even just asked him 1 question every week on the alphabet – he would have remembered. Then we could have really moved on to other exciting areas.

One thing I do is never throw out workbooks and make them write in pencil. This means I can rub out their answers and ask them to re-do the questions. It is like a new worksheet.

In Short

Periodically take some time out and help your children to revise.

REVISION: 10 Minutes every few weeks.

21. #TECHNOLOGY HAS ITS PLACE?

Computer apps are the most recent technological change. It is interactive, in colour and you have lots of apps at your finger tips. It can be a useful tool to help teach your child. However you have to search through a lot of apps or computer games before you find the right educational game that is appropriate for your child's level. To be honest, I have searched a lot and I still haven't found a good app that is aimed at the right level or an app they haven't got bored of after the first few days. It would be good if I could find an app that grows with your child. Even if you pay for it, I am not so convinced.

At the end of the day, technology:

- Does not know what level your child is at.
- It does not know your child's strong points and hence allow them to skip over that point.
- It does not know your child's weak points and change to practise more of that.
- It does not adapt to your child's changing needs. No matter how whizzy the program is.

You as a parent can provide all the above compared to the app. It might be all right for a short period, but that is about it. All that time you took searching for it, trying it, paying for it, you could have spent it on your child and they could have learnt something!

There is an article I read [8]and it said that technology at school such as computers did not effectively teach your child core

---

[8] From http://www.bbc.co.uk/news/technology-18105992

literacy skills; good old fashioned reading traditional books did.

Ask yourself are you downloading these apps to babysit your child or are you getting it to actually teach your child? Use it in moderation but don't use it to replace your time with your child.

You will find that as the child gets older, they will be overcome with technology. It's the way of the world right now! Technology is even taking over my life. So I suggest you limit it as a child, but then allow them to use it in moderation and safely as they get older.

In Short

Just get on with spending some time with your child and save yourself the hassle. If you do find a good app then use it in moderation.

LOST TIME ON SEARCHING FOR THE RIGHT APPS: Days!

INVEST IN YOUR CHILD INSTEAD: 10 Minutes per day.

22. #LET'S TAKE SOME TIME AND LISTEN!

Did you know that the best coaches in the world actually just listen and then guide their counselees to come up with a solution themselves? The solution is often held within ourselves, and it just takes a series of logical questions and the right guidance to work out the solution. I have noticed that this is something that health visitors also do. They give you some tips on how to resolve the issues, but they never force it on you. They leave it up to the parent to take action based upon the tips that they provided.

The point of this tip is that we should listen to our children regularly and find out what they are doing at school or how they are feeling in general. For any issues that they may face, we should ask them a few logical questions to guide them in the right direction. This is to help them find a resolution for themselves, almost like a coach. The best course of action will be the one that they came up with in the first place and not always the solution that we have bestowed upon them. This is effective because we all have different mannerisms and different styles of working.

We should talk to our children on our walk back from school, over dinner, or even when they are playing. Listen to what they say. Listening to your children gives you a good insight into what they are weak on, what they are struggling with and of course what they are good at. My daughter sometimes brushes off chats, but it's sometimes worth digging a bit deeper and working out what exactly she has been doing at school and how things are going generally. The idea behind this is so that you can strategise and teach them this subject at home to give them a head start.

Listening is a skill within itself. This is a skill that is more important than ever before, especially since parents are more so addicted to their smart phones. Listening means looking at your child when they are talking to you, stopping whatever you may be doing at the time, empathising, repeating what they just said - so they can confirm you heard right. Listening can also be watching their body language. Sometimes children cannot articulate their views or express their feelings and body language might say it all especially when your child is not happy. So put that phone down for 2 minutes, ensure that you are really listening and give your full attention.

Children generally talk more about their friends or events that happened in school, more than their school work. My daughter sometimes tells me about how other classmates have been mean to her. I am sure this is a common conversation piece all parents have with their children. As I have said before academia is not everything. Unless you help your child has this issue, then academics is the least of your worries. I often just sympathize and agree that it was mean, if it truly was. However there have been times when she has mentioned it a few times and it's obvious then that she needs help. I'm no bullying expert however my plan of action to help a child for a non serious issue is: -

1. Advise your child how to avoid the scenarios
2. If they have to be in this scenario, then I provide some tips on how to prevent the bullying.
3. If it is still happening ask them to tell the teacher
4. If is STILL happening, then that's when you need to step in and talk to your teacher yourself.
5. Agree a plan of action with the teacher
6. Monitor and review and go back to point 3.

My personal view is that it is better to deal with the situation by points 1 and 2 (meaning by themselves), and then maybe 3. Often children go through phases and so you will probably find that it will eventually pass and I would give it a good amount of time on point 3 before you go to step 4.

If it is serious then you need to go straight to step 4 and do whatever it takes to help your child.

This tip is especially valid for older kids. Your job as the parent is to check in with them regularly and ask them what they need. This is especially when you have been preoccupied and haven't been in tune with what they have been doing lately.

One of the best times to talk to your children is when you are sat down to eat, usually breakfast, lunch or dinner time. I appreciate it may not happen every day, due to work schedules, but it should happen most days in a week. Eating as a family has great benefits. Not only does the family get a chance to bond and communicate with each other, but it also fosters a sense of belonging.

In Short

Listen to your child. Give them a head start with areas that they are studying on in school. For any issues: Act like a coach and work together with your child to come up with a plan of action to resolve it.

LISTEN TO YOUR CHILDREN: 5 Minutes per day.

23. #LET THEM ASK QUESTIONS

It is so important to let your children ask questions. What I always say is that every question is a valid one. Most questions you should be able to answer, however there will come a time when they get you with a real corker; whether it is a question that is not appropriate for their age or one you simply don't know the answer to.

If it is a rude question, I will let you decide on how to answer that question as ultimately you know your child best and it is up to you as a parent to decide how much you want your child to know and by when.

If it is a genuinely valid question and you don't know the answer then read the next tip. Remember most of the time there is no rush in answering it, so manage their expectation and admit you don't know the answer and tell them that you will get back to them later. If you find it hard to admit you don't know the answer (as I notice some people do) something like, "I'm not fully sure what the answer is, but it is a valid question, I will get back to you on that next week when I have time to just clarify a few minor points."

I noticed that the intelligent children in my school always had parents who could answer the questions, and took the time to do so.

All children are born curious, it is the natural way. So why not foster that inquisitive mind and give them the answers they need. It will boost their confidence and self esteem again. This will encourage them to aim high and challenge processes. A great skill if you want them to get ahead in their career!

My point is that we shouldn't brush off our kids with blank answers. We would not do that to an adult, so why do that to our children? Our children should deserve the same attention and respect as other human beings who asked the question. If we treat our children with maturity, then they will behave with maturity.

In Short

Let them ask questions and take some time to answer it.

ANSWER A QUESTION: 5 Minutes every so often.

24. #IF YOU DON'T KNOW IT, GOOGLE IT

Now there will be times, when your children come to you with questions and subjects which you don't know. My curriculum is totally different to my children's curriculum, so there is no doubt there will be areas that your kids learn, that you have never learnt and vice versa of course. Times have also changed, so new learning content has arisen. So if in doubt, Google the subject! The internet is a great resource. If your child is old enough, then they can search for it themselves. You can even buy books on it or get books from the library. I have had to search for things like how to do long division and how many wives Henry the VIII had. YouTube is also great, as it makes learning so much easier with video clips.

In Short

If you don't know it, Google it!

GOOGLE IT: 5 minutes when you need to

25. #FIND OUT WHAT'S NEXT ON THE LEARNING PLAN

When we are trying to get our children ahead at school we have to be smart about it! I like to call it "smart parenting." Sometimes it not what your child knows, it's about strategy and "playing the game." For example, there is no point in learning extensively about Kings and Queens of England, if your child is not going to be studying this in their history lesson (unless it if for recreation purposes). Don't get me wrong it is good to learn about this and may help you in general knowledge for later life, but not something they should learn extensively unless it is on the curriculum or exam syllabus.

I personally have tried to look up the national curriculum, however after hours of searching; I never find anything concrete and anything you can make sense of. I guess this is what teachers have to learn in their teaching post graduate year– how to translate the curriculum. Even my child's school has a website where you can download the key stage 1 / 2 curriculum. Sadly it still doesn't help me, only because it is not specific, but also because I do not know where the teacher has got to.

If your child attends a good school, then every term they should send out a letter home that states all about the beautiful subject areas that they are going to learn over the term. Sometimes even that can be a bit too wishy washy for me. For items that I find that are not specific, I just ask the teacher at the next available opportunity. "What exactly will you be learning this term?" This way you know what is next on the learning plan and can start practising this subject at home. If you can't get hold of the teacher then your children may have an insight.

Here is an extract from the national curriculum for English comprehension for schools in England for my daughter's age.

Pupils should be taught to: [9]

- develop positive attitudes to reading and understanding of what they read by:
- listening to and discussing a wide range of fiction, poetry, plays, non-fiction and reference books or textbooks
- reading books that are structured in different ways and reading for a range of purposes
- using dictionaries to check the meaning of words that they have read
- increasing their familiarity with a wide range of books, including fairy stories, myths and legends, and retelling some of these orally
- identifying themes and conventions in a wide range of books

As you can gather, there are so many ways in which the teacher can teach the child the above targets. Unless you know what the teachers specific class plan is: For example what book they plan to read in class or what theme they may be studying in that term, then as parents we cannot put some effort in with our children to try and get them ahead.

In my experience I find teachers answers a bit vague. Like we will just be adding on from last term, or we need to focus on

[9] Copied from www.gov.uk website in May 2016

the depth of the subject. When I get vague answers, I just keep probing until I get a solid answer; like we will be learning about fractions and astronauts this term.

Whatever is next on your child's learning plan, it's time to start learning about it. Learning at home ahead of the class session gives them great confidence and boosts their self esteem. It will not hurt your child if he/she has learnt it already at home first. Take for instance: If your child has read a Shakespeare book at home already, then it will definitely help if they read it in class again. Utilise the SMART parenting term that we saw in #SET SOME GOALS.

In Short

Work out what's next on the learning plan, step into the details to learn it to stay ahead.

FIND OUT WHAT NEXT ON THE LEARNING PLAN: 5 minutes every so often

26. #WOULD YOU BELIEVE THAT YOU KNOW YOUR CHILD BETTER THAN THE TEACHER

This statement is so obvious, but one that parents need to be reminded of from time to time. We often look towards the teachers for some insight into how well our children are doing at school. However if you follow most of the tips in this book, you as the parents should really know all this. You are in control of your child's progress and you should use the teacher's comments as a confirmation of what you already know. They may fill you in on the little aspects, but you are the manager of your child. Don't get me wrong, it is still important to talk to the teacher so that you do not miss out on any key messages. I think this tip is a no brainer and as a parent you should know your child better than your teacher and take the lead in where your child needs to go.

In Short

You really do know your child the most, so take the leadership role and provide direction for your children.

KNOW YOUR CHILD: All the time.

27. #PUT SOME EXTRA TIME IN?

This tip seems to go against the grain of my book. What I mean by this is, when they get some homework get them to spend a bit more time than required on it and produce some exceptional work. Think outside the box.

Some say that a lot of homework can actually be done before you get home, maybe at school during some down time or maybe on the bus. For the most committed child, I would say do as much as you can in school so that you have time at home to get ahead or just hang out. I would suggest that your child doesn't overload themselves either and remind them that having breaks is good for them too.

My friend once told me that homework is just work that they have not had a chance to cover in class. It's not supposed to be a learning exercise more of a practise exercise. She believes it so much that she is not bothered if her son gets any homework or not. She thinks that it is actually great they don't get any homework, it actually allows her to teach him other things, things that she feels is more important. Maybe there is some truth in that?

Either way, doing homework above and beyond what is expected will gain you some extra brownie points.

When I was a child, I noticed if you were focused enough you could actually get your basic homework done in 10 minutes. Not much at all. And obviously it's best to just get it done in school or as soon as you get home, so your child can focus on enjoying themselves for the rest of the evening.

For larger homework activities, it is worth your child asking the teacher for some tips or what exactly the teacher is looking for, to gain the most marks. Some people like to call that "brown-nosing." This is something that business people are doing all the time. They link in with their managers, colleagues or clients to find out what they are looking for especially when applying for other jobs or trying to find a new marketing/sales opportunities. It happens all the time, so why not start them from young?

In Short

To go above and beyond and to produce exceptional work, your child will need to put in some extra time and effort.

PUT SOME EXTRA TIME IN: 10 Minutes now and then.

28. #TIME FOR SOME REWARDS

It is so important that your child doesn't get too engrossed in constant learning. We should allow them to take a break, reflect on achievements and give a reward. Whether it's a trip to the park, an ice cream, a trip to the cinema or buying a toy that they like. Hugs and praising is always a good reward. Rewards should come little and often but most importantly in a timely manner. There is no point taking them to the cinema for an achievement that they did 6 months ago, they will have probably forgotten what it was for. Take some time out, reflect and enjoy.

I just want to mention that ultimately the true reward for their hard work in their studies is the success that they will become. So saying things like: "If you pass your exams then I will buy you a games station (X-Box)", I am not convinced that that this is the right thing to do. At the end of the day, you know your children, and you know what is best. Therefore you should do what suits you. If you find that your child is ultra motivated when you say you will buy them a games station if they get good grades, then it may be worth doing (if you have the money of course). I have known some parents who buy items for their children before the results come out, because they got a good deal. Please do not be tempted to do this because if they fail, then you will most likely still get it anyway. Your children will see right through you. If you say something, stick to it!

Good employers also adopt this tip to keep their workers motivated. Studies have revealed that money rewards are short lived because it won't be long before workers want more. Instead employers adopt other strategies, such as praising employees publicly; allowing flexible working, bringing sweets and cakes into the work place, buying lunches, taking workers out for dinners, handing out rewards for achievements and bright ideas. As you can see, rewards don't need to break the bank and similar principles can be applied to children.

In Short

Make some time and celebrate your child's achievements.

TIME FOR REWARDS: Every so often.

29. #ENCOURAGE THEM TO BE INDEPENDENT

It is so important that you do not spoon feed your children. Maybe I have been so far, but that is because they are still young. I try to encourage my children to be independent in small ways so far, after all I won't be there for them all the time. You can teach them to be independent by doing a first example with them on a worksheet and then letting them get on with it by themselves. You can just ask them to do some reading on their own. I even encourage my 4 year old to be independent, by saying, "Why don't you practise writing this word, while I put the clothes out?" This helps loosen the apron strings. If they are not in the mood to do any work, then maybe you could ask them to complete it by the end of the day. You should give your children a reasonable amount of time to complete a task. We are not in the army, and we must not expect our children to do tasks in military time. Giving them time to get on with things themselves, hopefully should allow them to be creative and find their own style.

When I am at the office, I find that I work so much better when I don't have a manager sitting over me, advising me how to do my work. I often end up resenting them, not enjoying my work and not working to my best ability. When I am just left with a task, I always find creative ways of achieving the goal and because it is my work and my work alone, thus I am more positive about it. This makes me a confident, respectable and a trustworthy team worker. I think we have all been in this scenario and you all know what I mean. So give your child the space he/she needs to do their work creatively and independently, especially the older they get.

Once they get a hang of the independence thing, this should hopefully give you more time back in your diary and allow you to get on with other things.

In Short

Set your children on a task, walk away and encourage them to be independant learners.

ENCOURAGE THEM TO BE INDPENDENT: Some time gained back in your diary.

30. #BE CONSISTENT

As parents you must try to be consistent, and that way your children will act and behave consistently. Being consistent helps you reinforce good practises to maximise your children's potential. They say that if you make a change and stick with it for 30 days, it will just then become a normal habit.

I noticed that when you are consistent, your children don't complain as much and they are more likely to accept the routine without any fuss. My children have a great morning routine. They have until 7:45am to eat their breakfast. They have until 8am to get ready, and then they have until 8:30am to do what they want, like watch TV or do their final bit of homework. In fact that last 30 minutes is really for me to get ready. As I have been consistent with this routine since the start it works really efficiently for me. The children have accepted it and just get on with it. Another great tip for running an efficient morning, is to get as much done as you can, the night before, like pack your bags and make your lunches (like I discussed in the 'Get the basics right' chapter. Once you start rushing about in your morning routines and doing things last minute, this is when your day will go all pear shaped and you will lose the children's commitment to keep the routine smooth. A bad morning inevitably impacts the rest of your day negatively. It is all about being organised.

I am also consistent in asking them what they did at school on our way home. I also ask them to get on with their homework every day when they get a chance. As you can see things run a lot more efficiently if you are consistent.

This also applies to behavioural issues as well. Children should know where you stand when it comes to bad behaviour. This is one thing that schools are good at. We will talk about behaviour issues in "#NIP BEHAVIOUR IN THE BUD" tip because that is a subject all on its own

I appreciate there are some occasions, when things change and your routine goes out of the window. We are all human and that's fine too. Just try and get back on track as soon as you can, for everybody's sanity. Remember when the day runs efficiently, it means you can make the time to maximise your child's potential.

In Short

Get some good routines in place and be consistent to maximise your childrens potential.

BEING CONSISTENT: All the time.

31. #DIFFERENT TIMES OF THE DAY FOR OPTIMUM RESULTS

I don't know about you, but I find I work better at certain parts of the day. I am definitely a morning person. I like to get up and get everything done as soon as possible, leaving the rest of the day to do whatever I want. So with that in mind, I find I learn better in the mornings. Sometimes I find I work well after lunch too. So based on the fact that we should know our children the most, we should be able to work out what times our children work best for optimum results.

I find my daughter does not learn well just before bed time. She is often not in the mood and she doesn't absorb information very well. So based on this, I try and get my teaching done, early evening during school days and early in the morning on non school days to avoid near bedtime. I appreciate you can't exercise this tip everyday but it is good to work with your child at a time that suits both of you.

I read an article once which said that girls tend to work better in the morning and boys in the afternoon. I can see a little truth in that. They also said that different types of lighting can help achieve better results. In short, what they were trying to imply is that children in classrooms with brighter lighting got better grades, compared to children in classrooms with dimmer lighting. Also natural light worked best to improve behaviour, anxiety and stress and helped promote a better wellbeing. So a good environment can make a real difference. The Chinese call this "feng shui." My daughter seems to love learning in our home office. The natural lighting is good in there, the desk is clear, we have all sorts of stationery and there is always the home computer at hand as well. So experiment with your child's working area to ensure "chi" – a good positive energy is happening.

In Short

Use this knowledge to create a great workspace, find a good time to learn and watch your child work to their maximum

WORK AT THE RIGHT TIME OF DAY: Included as part of the 10 minutes per day regime.

32. #GET YOUR FAMILY ON BOARD

So you have your partner on board, now you should consider getting your family on board too, if applicable. You can even get your childminders on board too, if they are willing to give it a go. I say this because when children are of preschool age, they do spend a lot of time with grandparents or childminders. If you are like me a working parent, my parents used to look after my children while I was at work all day. In that time they can learn so much through play and focused effort, without being full on. So I would tell my parents to read books with them when they get a chance or practise numbers with them for example. When your children are being cared for by somebody else, why should all that time be dead time? It doesn't have to be too formal. I just throw one liners to my parents now and then.

As they get older, I find my parents only look after them in the school holidays. In that case I say "make sure Mia reads for 10 minutes today." It's better than watching TV all day or stuck on a games console! To be honest I am quite thankful that my parents are very active people, and with that the kids are also very active. My parents do all sorts with my kids, take them to the park, gardening, cooking, take them on bus rides, shopping and many more activities. All these things are learning opportunities. So for that I am truly grateful.

If you don't have the luxury of having grandparents nearby, then maybe it is worth asking your child minder or other family members if they look after your children. Childminders can only do this if they don't have many children to look after. I appreciate this may not be always possible. Like for example when my daughter was one, I put her in a private nursery part time. Just in the hope she would meet new friends and get to play with other things like painting and play dough. However I came to quickly realise that private nurseries that are not attached to schools do nothing really other than look after your child and cover their basic needs. Their primary job is not to teach your child. Even one of the nursery staff admitted that it is better to put your child in a school associated nursery than a private "looking after" nursery, as the school attached nurseries are more focused on learning.

I am lucky, my husband has some extended family around and my sister-in-laws are great. If ever I need help, I can ask them. I have invited them over to my house over the weekends to bake chocolate cookies with the kids. Once we went round to theirs and they helped my daughter make jewellery. So it's not always just about academia, it can be about practical skills too.

The message I am trying to get across here is to utilize the people around you to help you achieve your child's goals in a positive way. You should just have an informal agreement where every so often you throw one liners, like "Vinnie needs to practise his alphabet today" or "Mia has brought her workbook, it would be good if she gets a chance to do at least one page." If they get to do it that's great, if not it's no big deal.

In Short

Create a dream team, and get your family and babysitters to help out too.

ASK FAMILY AND BABYSITTERS TO HELP OUT: 1 Minute

33. #NIP BAD BEHAVIOUR IN THE BUD

Now we can't really teach our children anything and maximise their potential when behaviour is an issue. I personally don't really have any major behavioural issues with my children, but on some occasions we have had our moments. My approach to bad behaviour is:

1. Give them a warning, example "if you hit your sister again, I will have to put you on the thinking step because that is not very nice."
2. If they do it again, put them on the thinking step and explain why you have put them there. The number of minutes I put them there correlates to their age. Example for a 2 year old I would put on the step for 2 minutes and a 7 year old, I would put them on the step for 7 minutes.
3. Be persistent. If they move off the step, hold their hand with no eye contact and no comments and keep leading them to the step. Show them that you mean business.
4. Once they have genuinely sat on the step for the allocated time. I will go there and bob down to eye level and explain why I put them there again. I also talk about the implication of their behaviour. Sometimes at this point they are still not ready to admit that they did wrong. So I ask them to still sit there until they calm down and are ready to talk to me nicely again.
5. A few minutes later. I usually get a hug and an apology and we just move on.

This is a standard approach which I have seen on the Super nanny program. If you have not watched this programme before then try the Super nanny book by Jo Frost. I have heard great reviews on this book. I am sure there are other similar books out there too.

The key thing with nipping bad behaviour in the bud is to be consistent. We should not let them get away with bad behaviour one day and then pounce on them the next day. With my daughter, if I put her on the thinking step one day, I won't have to do it again for the next few years. She absolutely hates being in trouble and sees it as such a big deal. She is genuinely always good. In her 8 years, I think I have only put her on the thinking step less than 5 times. My point here is that once your children sees that you are serious about not accepting bad behaviour, they will think twice before they do it.

The other point I want to make is, as parents we should never make empty threats. Example, "if you be naughty today, you will not get to play the xbox all week," and then not stick to it. Trying to stick to threats is very hard, as we all know. Not sticking to threats is a trap that so many parents regularly fall into. Another example is, "if you eat this sweet, you can't eat more sweets for the rest of the day." It is difficult when you have more than one child because when the other child gets a sweet later on that day, the threat is impossible to keep to. In the end you do give up and give the naughty child another sweet. It is almost unfeasible to cope with their cute faces and your own guilt. It is better to say "if you are good all day, then I will give you a sweet." Giving at the end is a much better approach. Your child is cleverer than you think and can see right through those empty threats.

Proactive parenting is an approach I like to use, whereby you plan your day and communicate your expectations to your children, rather than being reactive to their not so good behaviour. For example, "If you be good all day then at the end of the day you will get to choose a treat" or "We are going to the zoo and there will be lots of walking to do. If you do well, we can get an ice cream after lunch." This should hopefully stay in the child's mind and they will try to behave well. It is good to set the child's expectation for the day, so they know what's happening.

This is similar to having a reward chart. Reward charts are fairly common nowadays, they are used by many professionals and you can even buy them from your local supermarket. Some parents are really creative and create their own reward charts for their children. When I say professionals, I mean teachers and even supernanny – Jo frost. I have used reward charts in the past; however for me it is short lived, because my children are good most of the time. I find it can be a useful approach to encourage good behaviour for both the long and short term. It can also be used for other things, like encouraging your children to eat their greens.

If you genuinely have a child that does not conform to normal good behaviours and you have given the Super nanny type advice a good go, then I am no child behaviour expert and I suggest you visit your GP. There could be some other factors contributing to the problem. It is worth seeking professional help in the hope that the situation will improve.

For some minor bad behaviour traits, you might just need to let it slide. For example I once read in a book about a professor who got kicked on the leg whilst talking to the child parents. He decided to ask the child to stop. At that point, all the child could think about was kicking the professor again in a moment of rebellion. As you can imagine the professor then got kicked a few more times before the parents really had to step in. In this instance, if the professor just ignored the kick, the child probably would not have done it again. We all live and learn. The child would have thought his action was boring, if he got no attention from it and would have moved onto something else.

If your child's teacher has approached you about behavioural issues at school, then I suggest you should support the teacher and help them, help your child. Let the teacher know that you agree and support what they are saying. Ask them if there is anything you can do at home to continue the discipline at home and ensure you follow through with it.

Teenagers are a different story and the thinking step probably does not apply to them. They will genuinely suffer mood swings due to the hormonal changes. I can't speak from experience just yet on teenagers, but as an outsider seeing other parents with teenagers I can give you some pointers.

It is hard to deal with teenage problems because as parents, you are constantly in the thick of it and it is hard to see the light at the end of the tunnel. Other than talking to them and the art of persuasion, my view is to just take a break, step back, and gain a prospective of the world.

All teenagers understand the consequences of their actions and will eventually see the light. Another tip is to talk to them about the body changes and how it can impact mood.

Acknowledgement is the first step. Giving them space can help and all that we can do is hope that they will eventually see your point of view. Talk about the good times you have, it can be an ice breaker in to getting to talk about the real issues. Getting another adult to talk to your child might help as well because in reality teenagers sometimes don't like talking to their parents.

In Short

Nip bad behaviour in the bud, no matter what your childs age is and be consistent, this will give you more time to execute the rest of the tips in this book!

NIP BEHAVIOUR IN THE BUD: Mandatory

34. #DON'T GIVE UP IN THE SCHOOL HOLIDAYS

Now I'm not a tiger mother and I am a big believer in taking breaks, however during the holidays when you have some time you should continue with your 10 minutes per day investment. For the short term time holidays, I don't really an much issue with. It is the long summer holidays where we should try and keep our children's brain active. There have been studies out there which suggest that pupils who take shorter but regular holidays do maintain their knowledge and perform better.

I can vouch for that. In my standard schooling where I had the long 6 weeks summer break, by the time I returned back to school again in September, I felt I had forgotten much of the things I had learnt previously. However, when I went to an academy college where they only gave you a 4 week summer break, I felt the momentum was there and the knowledge seemed a lot fresher.

When your child is on their own over the holidays, it can be hard to strive up the motivation to do anything. However with you as parents on their side, you can help keep your child's momentum going. Hopefully your child should feel more motivated and keep up the good work.

In Short

Continue with you 10 minutes per day in the holidays.

IN THE HOLIDAYS: Continue with the 10 minutes per day

35. #SURROUND YOUR CHILDREN WITH A GOOD BUNCH OF FRIENDS

You would think this subject is a small one; however there is some great truth in this. All the top entrepreneurs say this and the same should apply to your children to get the best of out of them.

In my daughter's class, there are not many classmates that really push her, probably because she has been top of her class since she first started school. One particular year a new boy joined her class and his maths was impeccable. He was getting tested on his maths targets weekly, whereas all the other children on average were getting tested half yearly. When my daughter saw that targets could be achieved weekly as opposed to fortnightly, she felt the need to push herself. If he could do it, so could she. I said nothing during this time because my belief was that a child should know their content thoroughly, before they get tested. This is what I had been told by the teachers, who sometimes tested the children three times over a six week period to ensure they really knew their content. Either way, my daughter put a little bit more focus on her math targets and she too was then passing her targets week on week. So it just goes to show that, if she was surrounded by more children who do well then she would definitely go further.

I believe you should send your kids to a school where they will be surrounded by good and happy children. The general positive behaviour and pace of learning should rub off on each other, to make them great children. This is not just something to think about with schools, it also applies to children who live on your street and the ones that go to the same clubs as yours.

I have a lovely window cleaner. He always complains that the school his son goes to is not great and has somehow got into the wrong crowd. If he had the money he would definitely move his son to another school in the hope he will make a new set of friends.

I also know some ladies, whose children go to a different school. Not only are the children best friends, but the parents of those kids are also great friends. They even go on holiday together, and they have all turned into school governors together. So collectively they are prosperous and doing their best to make their school a great place to be. So when you have a great team working together like that, it can only bring everyone forward together.

Think about the people you spend your time with, like co workers, family and friends. You will notice that pessimistic people are like parasites and sap the goodness out of you. I notice myself sub consciously backing away from negative people. I think I do this because I came from a hard working family who were positive and believed in hard work without complaining, hence I don't like it. I also recognise that it leads to negativity and I just don't want that. I believe in the Barack Obama "can do" attitude, because you really can achieve things when you put your mind to it.

I appreciate that this tip is not the easiest to follow. Sending your kids to a school, where the children are well behaved is a start. Maybe you can limit your kid's interactions with the unhelpful children if possible. If they find good friends, remind them that they are good friends. This tip is a tricky one to achieve especially when the odds may be against you, but it's good to know and to keep trying. Even as an adult, I try to join the right groups and mingle with the right people to help me achieve my goals. A director of a large company once told me that "it's not always what you know, it's who you know." Knowing good fellow pupils and people should lead to good opportunities and make your children push themselves to achieve greater results.

"Walk with the dreamers, the believers, the courageous, the planners, the doers, the successful people with their heads in the clouds and their feet on the ground" – Wilfred Peterson

In Short

Surround your children with other good children and together they will prosper.

SURROUND YOUR KIDS WITH OTHER GOOD KIDS: All the time

36. #KEEP THEM MOTIVATED

There is no definitive answer to this tip. Here are some sub tips that will help:

- Making subject's fun is always a start. Talk with passion and be positive.
- Breaking big subjects into smaller manageable areas always helps.
- You can celebrate past achievements and talk about how difficult it was and remind them what success felt like. It could have been a certificate or even congratulations from someone.
- Eliminate any repetitive talking (nagging). This is such a drainer.
- Allow your children to do activities that they actually enjoy.
- Consider rewards. However rewards are short lived.
- Talk to your children and work out why they don't enjoy it, or why they have lost their motivation. Try to ask your child to come up with a solution to fix it or fix it yourself if that doesn't work. #LETS TAKE THE TIME TO LISTEN/COACHING
- Accept your child may not be good at something and move onto something else. Don't be too much of a perfectionist.
- Let them be as creative as they like when learning the subject.
- Praise their efforts, no matter how small it may be.
- Let them fail? This is a tough one to allow. However from some failures there comes great determination to be a success.

I am thankful that I don't have an issue with this tip, most likely because I use my 50 tips in variation, I teach with passion and my children love learning.

In Short

Use all or some of the sub tips and hope that your children get motivated.

MOTIVATE YOUR CHILD: A part of your 10 minutes a day.

37. #DON'T ACCEPT – YOUR CHILD IS DOING OK

Parent consultation evenings are so important. As a parent, it is a mandatory requirement that you attend your child's parent's evenings. Most parent consultation evenings for me, start with the teachers saying "they are doing ok." I don't know if this is the standard answer or whether they just don't have enough energy left at the end of the day. You need a bespoke answer in order for you to work out a plan to help your child, so don't accept everything is ok. There is always room for improvement. Before I go to parent's evenings I always jot down questions I want to ask. (There has been a time, where the teacher just talks and talks and you can't get a word in edgeways!)

Here are a few questions I like to ask:

- What can he/she do to improve?
- What will he/she be learning next?
- What do you feel are their weaknesses?
- Is there anything she could do better?
- Is there anything he/she can do to make her work stand out above their peers?
- Are there any behavioural issues that I need to know about?

These questions probe the teacher into providing more of a bespoke answer. Sometimes I have noticed that the child's school report is often standard text. I don't blame them in a way because they do have lots of reports to write.

Don't wait for parents evening either, if you have concerns. Strike up regular conversations with the teacher and talk to them regularly. Tell them what you want. If you can't chat to them or you feel you are not getting the message across then write a note to them. A good teacher should appreciate good feedback. Talk to the teacher with your concerns. Don't just tell them the problems, tell them the solution or ask them to come up with a solution.

In Short

Don't accept your child is doing ok. Ask the teacher how your child can improve and get specifics.

ATTEND PARENT CONSULTATION EVENINGS: 30 min- utes per term

38. #KEEP THE TEACHERS ON YOUR SIDE

Teachers can be wonderful people and a key aid to help your child progress and achieve. So it is so important to keep them on your side. You don't want to annoy them, so they subconsciously make your child's life miserable. Be friendly with them as they can open up and offer suggestions/tips on the next steps of your child's development. Talk to them regularly because progress is made in small and regular steps. I have heard teachers admit that they are more likely to push a child, when they have the support of the parents behind them.

One issue I have with schools in England is that they are so standard and they are bounded by government guidelines. The teachers are so stuck to the syllabus that they sometimes cannot think above and beyond it. This means that any feedback you give as a parent is either ignored or it takes so long to adopt. Don't get me wrong, minor points are usually taken on, but bigger issues can be a pain to take on.

One of my daughter's pet hates is when the rest of the class slows her progress or one or two kids in her class doesn't follow the rules, so everyone gets punished for it. I can agree with her on that one. That is just so unfair to the rest of the class especially if it is the same culprits every week! If you are a teacher reading this, please take note of this and be fair to the good students. ☺

If you have some spare time and believe you can make a difference in your child's school, then it is definitely worthwhile to do it. Whether you are a parent governor or even if you volunteer. Schools are great community hubs, and add so much more value when there is a good set of parents organising activities, such as summer fairs.

Below are a few ideas on how you get involved with your child's school. Bear in mind, you are also demonstrating leadership abilities and a team work spirit, when getting involved and let's hope it rubs off on the children.

Parents can get involved by:

- being a classroom helper
- organizing and/or working at fundraising activities and other special events, like bake sales, car washes, and book fairs
- chaperoning field trips
- attending school board meetings
- joining the school's parent-teacher group
- reading a story to the class
- giving a talk for career day
- attending school concerts or plays

Whatever you choose to do, make sure you enjoy it and remember it all adds value.

I do like the idea of parents presenting their careers to school children. It would give children a great insight into real life careers firsthand. Schools should adopt this once a year and make this an annual fixture. If they don't have enough parents with good jobs, then they should ring up organisations, and get somebody in to do a talk. Places like police stations, hospitals and hairdressers etcetera. After the presentation, they can maybe do activities that replicate the careers that were talked about. Surely this can only be a good thing.

In Short

Get involved with your childs school, add some value and make a difference. Together you can all move ahead.

GET INVOLVED IN SCHOOL: Whenever you can.

39. #GROUND YOUR CHILDREN?

When I say ground your children, I don't mean keep them in their rooms all week because you are mad at them or they have done something wrong! I mean ground them in the sense of reminding them that there are lots of children in the world who do not have the same opportunities as us and for this we should be thankful. There are children who are starving in this world and they walk for miles just for a few litres of water. They don't even go to school.

The best way to probably ground your children is by doing some charity work, if you have the opportunity. I am not going to lie to you and say I have done this before. I wish I could find a safe local charity I can help out with occasionally. The idea is that my children will be able to see firsthand, how unfortunate other people are and how fortunate they are.

Also we must remind our children to help out around the home. We all live together and we must all work together to create a good and clean environment at home. I am personally not a fan of giving children pocket money for doing household chores. Not just because you will be out of pocket every time you ask your children to do a chore, but it means they don't ask "What will I get in return?" every time you ask them to do something!

Most importantly it is important to say thank you, when your children help out in the house or wherever. If they are persistent and choose not to help, then I suggest you don't knock them and just be a role model and show them how to do it. Eventually through guilt, they may see the error of their ways. Offering choices helps achieve the goal as well, like "would you like to empty the dishwasher or tidy your toys away?" The key thing is not to control them because we are not in the army and it is not a nice way to be treated.

Grounding your children gives your child some maturity, which is good for everyone all round.

In Short

Ground your children by asking for help around the house, and teaching them that they are really fortunate.

GROUND YOUR CHILDREN: 5 Minutes per day.

40. #NOT PROGRESSING?

Do not get hung up if your child is not progressing. A new approach may need to be adopted. It happens to all of us at times. If this is happening, the first thing I do is check with my husband to see if he has been teaching the child the same subject. I find that if we are both teaching a child a subject but we are using two different methods, this can seriously lead to big confusions. There are lots of different ways to teach a subject. For example, my son hated sitting down and watching educational DVD's. Instead I tried counting numbers and teaching him to spell whilst kicking a foot ball.

If you have tried other methods and you are simply not getting anywhere, I would consider just dropping the subject for a while and coming back to it later, if possible. Or you can even just let the teacher go over it; after all they are supposed to be the experts. For older children, it may be worth getting a tutor in. Sometimes things just need time, and eventually it will just click into place, for your child. Remember to praise them for their efforts and to stay positive.

In Short

Use other techniques or just take a break, eventually they will get it.

USE ANOTHER TECHNIQUE: 10 Minutes per day
OR TAKE A BREAK: Zero time

41. #DON'T CHECK OUT AS YOUR CHILD GETS OLDER

As your children get older, it is so easy to check out and let them get on with things. So the action we must take here is to check in with our older children regularly. I recommend daily or weekly, depending on their maturity and ability. Find out what they are learning at school and the challenges that they are facing and help them by plugging in any gaps; by whatever means necessary or by using some of the other tips in this book.

In Short

Stay in tune, and stay checked in.

STAY CHECKED IN: 5 Minutes per day

42. #FOR OLDER KIDS WHO ARE DOING EXAMS

My advice for parents of older children who are doing exams is:

1. Find out what is on the syllabus for that subject
2. Work out which areas your child is good and weak at
3. Work with your child to attain more knowledge on the weaker areas
4. Set some learning goals and review regularly
5. Don't forget to practise what your child is good at as well, we don't want the child to neglect any skills
6. Start early and revise regularly.

All the above points are obvious. One of my key tips is to not wait until the teacher gives you old exam papers to practise. If your child has a teacher like what I had then they will give you a few papers to practise ahead of the exam which can sometimes be too late. Nowadays, you can download past papers on the internet, or buy books with past exam papers in them. It is a useful tool for parents and children to see what type of questions they ask. You should help your child strategise and teach them how to write answers in a way that will score the most points. Example: 1 point for the right answer and 3 points for the method.

I am currently giving my daughter 11+ question papers. Her success on these papers will determine which secondary school she will go to. I have noticed she can whizz through the maths questions, however she struggles a little with the English questions. As I have got these papers early, I now have 2 years to practise the English questions. This gives me plenty of time to teach her the subject, as opposed to me fretting and rushing at the end, especially with my busy work schedule.

Remember it is all about strategy and not always what you know. I would suggest that your child practises the papers again, near exam time to get them back into the swing of things and keep the strategy fresh in their minds. If your child can't work out the answers then allow them to start from the answer and work their way backwards.

If your child is really struggling with a subject and you feel you cannot help them, then maybe it is worth while getting a tutor in to teach your child. If your budget won't allow that, then talk to your child's teacher and see if they can help. I had an English Literature tutor to help me climb from a grade E to a B. I am so thankful my mum worked with an ex-English teacher and he did a really good job teaching me the Shakespeare classics. I was not doing so well in that class because there were 30+ students and one teacher, and I just was not getting any attention from the teacher. If he had come a bit earlier, I am sure I would have got an A.

To help reduce the stress of learning, as I have said before, break subject areas into manageable pieces, so goals are attainable in the 10 minutes per day regime.

In Short

Start early, work out your childs weak points and focus on them. Get your child practising past exam papers as early as possible.

START REVISING EARLY: Part of the 10 minutes per day.

43. #NEVER GET COMPLACENT

Don't get complacent. The minute you think your child is at the top, the reality is that they are not! No doubt other kids will come along to beat them. Keep up the momentum and don't lose it.

If you are struggling to work out what to teach your children next, then seek inspiration by looking at your child's curriculum or activity books. Ask the teacher, what your child could learn next.

This is something that all highly competitive, successful entrepreneurs believe in well.

In Short

Never be complacent, and keep the momentum going.

STAY IN THE GAME: Part of the 10 minutes per day regime

44. #LET YOUR CHILDREN DREAM BIG

Let your children dream big. Ask your children, what do they want to be when they grow up? In reality they don't know the full spectrum of jobs out there and they don't know the scope of the role, especially younger children. The truth is their career ambitions will probably change from week to week.

I occasionally ask my children, what they want to be. Currently my daughter wants to be a fashion designer. Who knows she may be the next Vivienne Westwood! She should be what she wants to be and she is also allowed to change her mind.

For children who don't know what they want to be, you can ask them "Who inspires you?" We should let them research these people and let them learn their story, in the hope that they gain inspiration from them. With the internet at their fingertips, this is such an easy thing to do.

If nobody or nothing motivates your children, then just allow them to do activities that they enjoy and hopefully time will give them an indication of what path to follow.

This tip is not just applicable to children; it also applies to us as adults. In fact I'm still a dreamer. When I read about these rich and successful people, they often start with one thing and one thing only. That thing is: They dreamt big. My motto now in life is: "Go big or go home!"

In Short

Let you child dream big and never knock their dreams.

LET YOUR CHILD DREAM BIG: ZERO TIME

45. #APPRENTICE STYLE ACTIVITES

For those entrepreneur type parents who want their children to follow in their footsteps, or for the non-entrepreneur parents; it is worth you setting up apprentice style activities for them. From setting up a basic lemonade stall, or letting them be creative and going for the big one.

I constantly ask my daughter to be creative and make something that she can sell. She always wants to make jewellery; however I feel her prototypes are never professional or fashionable enough to sell. I give her this feedback in the hope to improve her ideas, but the truth is she just hasn't got round to it. Honest and constructive feedback should help them think more deeply into the idea and provide a stronger path to follow.

I have heard apprentice style activities being done by secondary schools. In my opinion, I want to see more of this. I remember at my first school when I was aged around 8/9. I was lucky enough to be chosen by the teacher to stand with her in a second hand ornaments stall. I got to help her price up the items and take money from people. I don't know why, but I just loved it.

Entrepreneurs hold a true spirit of self determination. I really love the idea where you can make something at school and then sell it in a school crafts fare or using the internet. It can only be a good thing.

Below are some of the lessons that can be taught in apprentice style activities:

- Being creative. Brainstorming and developing ideas.

- Market researching. I.e. is this something that people will buy and is there any competition out there.
- Proto- typing. Creating a product or service.
- How to be unique and original.
- Leadership and strategy - the path the product goes to market.
- Pitching your ideas to a wider audience - presentation skills
- Market your product – advertising.
- Money – profit, loss and breaking even.
- Reviewing the experience and learning the lessons.

Children should be given the opportunity to try these apprentice style activities. It will give them the confidence to try new ideas.

Sometimes as an adult and through our own experiences we know that the ideas our children put on the table are going to fail. However if it costs nothing to try, then we should let our kids make their own mistakes. We should never say "I told you so" after the event. The best lessons are the ones that they learn for themselves. When lessons are learnt, the world will have more successful stories to tell.

The best designers/entrepreneurs have made products that have failed so many times, before they hit the right idea. James Dyson invented the cyclonic vacuum cleaner. It took him 5 years and many prototypes before he managed to produce something that actually worked and was viable to sell. He stuck to his idea, improved it on the go and now he is one of the most memorable inventors of our time.

Whilst doing these apprentice style activities, ensure your child know that they have the responsibility and it is their decision how they want to lead this. This is teaching your child about responsibility and leadership, it doesn't matter if they are not actually leading anybody.

There are so many stories of successful child entrepreneurs. One recent story that comes to mind is about a boy called Shubham Banerjee. He recently invented a low cost machine to print Braille for visually impaired people as part of his school project. He used a Lego Mindstorms EV3 play kit. He did some research and found out that normal existing Braille printers cost around $2000 each, which is really expensive in its own right, let alone for a person living in a developing country. His solution was really cheap at around $350 and weighs just a few pounds, compared with current models that can weigh more than 20 pounds. It was so good, that it impressed the executives at INTEL. They then decided to invest an undisclosed sum in his start-up. He was only 13 years old. [10]

Once you have completed the apprentice style activity, you should talk about the successes and the failures, and what you would do different next time. This will re affirm the lessons learnt and also provide better solutions for next time, if there is a next time.

Here are some examples of apprentice style activities that you can try with your children: -

- Lemonade stall at a fair or equivalent

---

[10] Story from https://en.wikipedia.org/wiki/Braigo

- Make something and sell it at a fair or on the internet
- Sell your old junk at a car boot sale, table top sale or on an Auction website.
- Buy something cheap and sell it at a higher price.
- Create a service, like washing people's cars or mowing their back lawn. I have known some children who have made a business out of it.

In summary, we should allow our children to be creative, and let them sell it to the world if they want, especially if the starts up costs are little or nothing. If they fail, it's not a big deal; at least they have learnt something and every failure will be a pillar to their success.

MONEY

While we are on the entrepreneurial theme, I just want to take a minute and talk about money. When I was a child, neither my parents nor the teachers really taught me anything about the big wide world and how money works: Things like getting a mortgage, insurance policies, loans, or gaining interest on your savings and shopping for the best deals. Money and Finance is such an important subject. Every single person needs to understand it and yet it was not taught at school. So much so that adults struggle with basic things like getting a mortgage. This subject is probably now on school curriculums, however as parents, it's best that you teach your children about money at home at some level. I would suggest when they are 10+. Simple principles on how interest on savings is calculated, or how you end up paying extra on loans borrowed. It is worth having the chat with them and ensure that they understand it by giving examples.

The key lesson that needs to be taught is about making certain that your children at least breakeven and then go onto making a profit. When the idea is laid out on the table with an estimation on gross revenue; and if your child realises that they will not even breakeven, then it is not worth doing the apprentice style activity (unless you have some other motivation to do this). If the numbers don't stack up, then it is simply not worth doing, unless your child can find a way to reduce the "running costs" or charge more money to make the numbers worthwhile.

I have read many business books on making money. The general theme of these books is that you need to save some money initially from your earnings and then you need to invest because "it takes money to make money." Obviously there needs to be an element of risk taking to invest. This is a key lesson you should teach your children, save initially and if you want your money to grow then you need to invest it.

The next story is an example of a child who saved initially and then went onto invest. Whilst watching YouTube a few months ago, I came across another child entrepreneur.[11] This girl was aged around 14 when she starting selling junk from her home on craigslist. She was doing relatively well that she even started asking all her friends for old toys and ornaments. She enjoyed it so much, she started going to garage sales to buy other items of value and furniture for next to nothing. By the time she was 15 or so, she had deposited $6,000 in her

---

[11] https://www.youtube.com/watch?v=GTTczC27fko

bank account. She then heard of a house on sale for $12,000 in a rundown neighbourhood in Florida, near where she lived (originally it was worth $100,000). Nobody really wanted to buy it, as it was small, in a rundown area and needed a lot of work, so she asked her mother for half the money to buy the home. As her father was a builder, she convinced him to help her do up the place. Thankfully all the jobs that needed doing were cosmetic and nothing structural. It took them 6 months, while her father cracked on and took on the harder work; she took care of the cosmetic work and cleaned the place up. Now she rents the place out for a $700 a month. Can you believe this? This child is truly inspirational. I tried selling items on eBay for money as a student, but I didn't think to go to the next level and buy cheap things from charity shops and car boot sales etc.

POCKET MONEY

Most children get pocket money. It is up to the parents to decide how much they want to give each child, or whether the children need to earn the money via household chores. Some studies have shown that boys get up to 12% more than girls. This surely can't be fair? It also states that boys are likely to ask for more money because they feel they deserve it.[12] This surprisingly echo's the current working world, where men get paid more for doing exactly the same job as women. We have come a long way with this and are so much better at

[12] Attained from the news article
http://www.bbc.co.uk/news/uk-36442389

equality, however there is still more work to be done. Despite so much attention this subject is getting nowadays and the government trying hard to reduce this. I can't help but feel that this is still happening, maybe not as much as before. I commend all the efforts that developing countries are taking to ensure that both men and women are treated fairly and that any pay gaps is removed.

The lesson I have learnt from this, is that the un-equality is developing at some level from a young age. So it is so important (coming from a parent of a girl) that you teach your children, girls especially that they should ask for more money, pocket money or at work. If they work hard, then they DO deserve the money! Be wary of what other people are earning around you and ensure that you are treated fairly and they earn the same money as similar counterparts around them. We should teach young girls to be strong, and not to see this as a conflicting issue, but more of a negotiation task.

From the training experience I have had through work; to enable women workers to progress up the career ladder. I was told that women often see asking for more money as a conflicting situation and hence they try to avoid it. Instead they should see it as a negotiation situation, where it is a problem that needs to be solved. When women/girls see this situation as a problem, then they can work through it and resolve/negotiate the issue.

EDUCATION TEACHES YOU TO IGNORE YOUR GUT, BUT SOMETIMES YOU NEED TO LISTEN TO IT.

Carrying on with the entrepreneurial theme, I just want to put this statement out there. Education teaches you to ignore your gut, but sometimes you need to listen to it.

Sometimes education tells us to ignore our gut feelings. Education teaches us to strategise, take calculated risks and formalise plans, and thus ignore our gut feelings. Do remind your child, that sometimes it's ok to listen to your gut feeling, take a risk and implement. Some of the top entrepreneurs have followed their gut instincts and have been successful. They may just stumble upon a great idea.

People who are successful are persistent, they are curious; they are challengers, optimistic and confident. We should instil these ideas, skills and values in our children.

"A quitter never wins and a winner never quits"

In Short

Mock up some apprentice style activites, watch your child deliver and learn the lessons.

MOCK UP AN APPRENTICE ACTIVITY: 5 Minutes on occassion.

46. #WHATS HAPPENING IN THE WORLD?

Occasionally I like to talk about what is happening in the world to my children. Sometimes my children ask questions when they catch snippets of the news. It is good for them to know what is happening in the world for general knowledge purposes and also some of that information can be applied to their school work. I often summarise happy occasions from the news for them. For example, "this year we are having the Olympics and it is going to be set in Rio de Janeiro, Do you know what country that is in?" Or "Today the American people are going to vote for the next president of United States of America. Barack Obama is the current president and now he is stepping down. He has been president for 8 years."

There are so many news items we can talk about. The best ones are the inspiring stories like the Canadian boy who recently discovered a lost Mayan civilisation. He had a passion for history and he was determined to find other historical Mayan towns. When we talk with passion, children tend to ask more questions on the subject and you can have interesting conversations. Another inspiring news item is the story about Leicester City Football team winning the premier league title. At one stage of the 2014-2015 season they were bottom of the league and were at risk of becoming relegated. They managed to survive, but again were one of the favourites to be relegated the next season. They then changed managers and with odds of 5000-1, they performed outstandingly and miraculously went on to win the league. It is an amazing story about a true underdog team being at the bottom, but through shear passion, determination and adversity, they fought to get to the top.

I tend to avoid the depressing war news stories because I want my children to live their life and not worry about the sad events that are happening in the world, certainly not as children. Keep it short, sweet and simple.

Talking about the world is a great conversation piece, and helps your child develop their thoughts and ideas. Originally I had this tip included as part of this book because if my parents talked with me about the news, then I would have done so much better at my general studies exam. However, children in England no longer have an opportunity to take this exam anymore.

Talking about the weekly news with your children will make them look super smart in school.

In Short

Talk with your children about the news that is happening in the world especially the happy and inspiring ones.

TALK ABOUT THE NEWS: 5 Minutes per week

47. #LANGUAGES

Languages are so important in this small world that we live in. It used to be a big world but the internet has changed all that. My first advice is that if you speak a different language at home, then as a family you should always try and speak it at home. Children have a great ability to pick it up at home. It's so much easier to learn a language at a younger age. Language receptors are really good on children under the age of 5. Based on all this I think schools should start teaching kids other languages from reception. Maybe not reading and writing but definitely speaking. Apparently it exercises a unique part of your brain which keeps people smart.

After meeting people from Mumbai - India, I noticed that they tend to speak quite a few languages fluently. They are so on the ball. I suspect it is because Mumbai is such a diverse place with so many different types of Indians living there. Some of my cousins speak up to 5 or 6 languages relatively fluently, Hindi, English, Gujarati, Marathi, Punjabi, Urdu and possibly others. It helps living in a diverse environment.

Some people seem to brush off languages as not important. I seriously disagree with this. I personally speak some Spanish – enough to get me by. It has helped me a great deal when I have visited places, like Cuba, Mexico, Spain and California. Yes I said California. I once got lost there and the only people around were some wonderful Mexicans. I simply asked "¿Donde esta Highway 405?" (Where is Highway 405?) They gave me some directions and I was back on my way again. So language is definitely useful especially for avid travellers like me.

Nowadays Mandarin seems to be a key language to learn, especially with our increased trading deals with China. If your child has some capacity, I would consider looking on YouTube or the internet to start learning a language. Learning a language will help your child bond with people around the world and improve their analytic and interpretive skills. It makes them open minded, impressive, develop confidence, improve their employability prospects and you never know they may even need it one day!

In Short

Start learning a new laguage, the younger the better.

LEARN A NEW LANGUAGE: Part of the 10 minute per day.

48. #THE TRAVELLING EXPERIENCE

Travelling the world is truly a magnificent experience for children. If you have the money then going abroad and learning about culture, languages, history, food and people can provide children a great learning insight. This is something that cannot be taught sitting in a classroom.

Attendance at school is very important, and where possible children should be taken on holidays during the holidays. Good attendance at school is linked to better achievement. However **in my personal opinion**, I feel that schools should allow parents to take their children out of school for a few days either side of the holidays, if they are genuinely going on cultural/learning holidays and where the child's attendance record is above 95%. I'm not so lucky with this respect. I live in an area whereby if you take your child out of school with unauthorised access, you get fined £60 per day, per child, per parent. So if I took both my children out of school for 1 day, my husband and I would get fined a whooping £240 a day. I feel the schools should be independent thinkers and show a little leniency for hard working children, who have a good attendance record. I know some people who can't even take their children on holiday in the school holidays, firstly because of the price and secondly due to work commitments. I would love to take my children to lots of countries: My list is endless. Wherever I take my children, I am sure they will at least learn something!

I want to tell you a story about a man whose lifelong ambition was to run the Boston marathon. He was seriously ill for some time and felt his dream was never going to be realised. He somehow miraculously got better, and decided to wait no longer and take his family out to Boston. He only wanted to take them out for one week to run the Boston marathon and also learn about the history of Boston. To cut a long story short, the school would not authorise his children's leave because of their policy on term time holidays. This was truly saddening considering his personal circumstances. He decided to take them out anyway, against the school's wishes because life is too short and he could not miss this opportunity. The key message he was trying to relay to the school, is that this was not just a holiday. It is a life changing experience where the children would learn about determination, passion, meeting your goals and history of the Boston tea party. (The children were going to learn about that anyway later in the school year) He argued that the one week trip to Boston would teach them more than a year at school. Ok, I would question that but I think he has a very fair point.

School trips are great for learning too. Looking back to my childhood, I remember all my school trips and what I learnt vividly.

"Life is not measured by the breaths you take, but by the moments that take your breath away."

In Short

If you have the money and the opportunity then travel the world with your children.

TRAVEL THE WORLD: Ok thats definitely more than 10 minutes per day, but your children are going to love it!

FINAL TIPS

49. #SETTING THE SCENE - CAN WE LEARN SOMETHING FROM THE FINNS?

As I have mentioned before, Finnish children do better at school compared to their European counterparts. Finnish teenagers are amongst the smartest in the world and they also say Finnish workers are the most productive. Over the course of writing this book, I have read lots of articles about this subject and below I have tried to summarise why they are so successful. 13

In Finland, children start school at the age of 7, so by this stage they are keen to learn. In their early years they get lots of 1-2-1 attention from their immediate family and that should give them a great start to school. They often have a 4 hour school day, in a relaxed and informal atmosphere. The rest of the day they are encouraged to play, be creative and have friends. I often see images of kids playing in the forests after school. Finnish parents allow their children to be more independent, and they just let their kids go to school by themselves.

Older Finnish students, rarely get more than a half an hour of homework a night. They have no school uniforms or classes for higher achievers.   There is little standardized testing at schools. Finnish Teachers are left to their own devices and have tremendous amount of freedom. Unlike England where schools are very standard and follow a strict curriculum. Teachers create lessons to fit their students and for younger

---

13 Information derived from article
http://www.wsj.com/articles/SB120425355065601997

children, they have the same teacher for 5 years or so. Teaching is a prestigious career in Finland. Teachers are highly valued and teaching standards are high. Schools are basic and they don't encourage extracurricular activities, even sport.

One of the reasons why Finnish students maybe successful is because of their love of reading. Parents of newborn babies receive a government-paid gift pack that includes a picture book. Some libraries are attached to shopping malls, and a book bus travels to more remote neighbourhoods. Finnish parents obviously claim some credit for the impressive school results. There is a culture of reading with their children at home and families have regular contact with their children's teachers.

Although we can't always adopt the Finnish lifestyle, as we all live in different cultures and some of us are bounded by government education policies; but you can see and feel the difference in their way of life. Maybe we can take a leaf out of their book and adopt some of the lifestyle changes at home?

In Short

Lets take a leaf out of the Finns book.

ADOPTING THE FINNISH CULTURE: All the time.

50. #GET SOME FRESH AIR

Fresh air is good for you as it helps clean the lungs and bring more oxygen to the cells. More oxygen also brings greater clarity to the brain, and when you breathe fresh air you can automatically think better, compared to rattling your brain indoors.

After all this reading, I suggest you and your children get some fresh air. Fresh air really helps you gain perspective, doesn't it? While you are out there, I want you to think about all the tips in this book and work out how to adopt them into your lifestyle and make that change. Remember if you make the change and invest in your children for at least 30 days, then your change will become a natural habit. Your children are what YOU make them, so take some time out now and ask yourself "what are my child's goals?" Scribble them down somewhere for starters and work out how you plan to help your child meet those goals.

Isn't that fresh air so good? OK what are you waiting for, start that 10 minutes now.

In Short

Get from fresh air, adopt a strategy and start that 10 minutes now.

START THAT 10 MINUTES NOW!

Ok, this is not the end of my tips. I have a bonus tip on keeping your children safe with technology just because I have attended some courses on keeping your child safe in the cyber world. Please read on.

#MY ADVICE ON TECHNOLOGY

Computer games and devices are everywhere. It will be inevitable that you will have to buy your children the latest technology at some point. Only because "all the other kids have it" and you don't want your children to miss out!

My initial advice is delay it, delay it and delay it as much as possible. This is because when they don't have it, they seem to live without it better. My 4 year old keeps asking me for an xbox and I have told him "I WILL buy it but when you are a bit older." The "I WILL" in the sentence, seems to calm him down and provides reassurance that I am reasonable, I don't want him to miss out and he will eventually get it. If I say "No, you can't have it," then the determination and fighting will set in and then life becomes so much harder. The delay rule also applies to social media. The legal age for children to use sites such as Facebook is about 13 anyway.

My second tip is never let these games consoles enter their bedrooms. I have learnt from other parents that once it is in the bedrooms, it is never coming out especially during exam times. There will be a big battle if it ever has to come out. The major problem with putting technology in your children's bedroom is that you cannot monitor your child's on these devices. Whether it is in relation to how long they have been on it or what exactly they have been doing on it. Gaming devices, computers and social media can be very addictive nowadays. This point also applies to having televisions in children's bedrooms. As a parent if there was a TV in my child's bedroom, I would be concerned that they might have the temptation to switch the TV on late at night when programmes are in appropriate.

When you do eventually buy these devices, set some rules and stick to it. A weekly chart, which shows when they can play their games, might be a useful idea. This way there is no doubt and the child clearly knows the rules. I would suggest maybe weekends only, but as a parent you are the best judge of this. The reason why I don't say daily is because of the addiction point. You should set some technology free days to ensure that your children do not get hooked. On my cyber safe training course, I was told that some children have been doing silly things to cheat their way to higher levels on games. When I say silly, I mean really silly; so much so that it has cost lives. Apparently it can be more addictive than smoking.

I know one particular work colleague, who has no technology day for his whole family every Sunday. This means no TV, no computers, no tablets and no gaming. They spend their Sundays as a family, talking, playing board games, going for walks and reading. It may seem a little extreme, however it works for them and they seem all the better for it.

If you are struggling to manage the time that your children are spending on computer tablets, then there are apps out there that can help. It can limit your child's use on the device and also monitor which sites/apps they have been using and for how long. Another way you can ensure that they are not sneakily going on the internet at certain times of the day is by switching off your broadband hub, especially at night.

Another tip I have for parents is to ensure that you fully supervise children and do not get distracted by your smart phones. I have mentioned this because I have heard increasing stories about children being in serious incidents because parents have got distracted by the beeps on their smart phones. It is so easy to do. My suggestion would be to only check your phone 3 times a day at set times, unless it rings. Put you phone in a drawer when you get home. I refer to it as "smart working" to utilise your time better and ensure you provide your children with the real quality time that they deserve.

There is so much advice on the internet these days about how to keep your children safe on the internet. You should take the time and implement these ideas because there really is a deep dark side to the internet. Remember, once your child posts something on social media, that post is out of their control and that is a key message we must teach our children. However you choose to manage your child with technology, keep them safe!

PART III

IF YOU ARE A TEACHER

If you are a teacher and you are reading this, I hope you agree with these tips for starters. It would be good that you regularly send out letters to the parents and share some of my tips with them and emphasize the 10 minutes a day principle. In the hope that together we can make a difference and raise standards.

WHAT SUCCESS LOOKS LIKE

Below are a few examples of how you know your children are ahead in school and that you know you are doing a great job as a parent.

- Your child being happy.
- Teacher praising your child at parent's evenings or at any other opportunity.
- Good school reports.
- Achieving goals.
- Gaining certificates and trophies.
- Children coming home with good grades on their work
- Children telling you how well they did on a piece of work.
- Children passing exams.
- Children presented with good school opportunities or a good university offer.
- Children to young adults getting good jobs.
- Finally children finding their passion and achieving their goals.

#EXPECT SUCCESS

This tip I have left for the end of the book. As parents you should expect success from your children. The reason why I say this is because your children will have the confidence to achieve.

Before I passed my driving test, my father's attitude was simply – it's too easy, you are a good driver, as soon as you have taken the test you will pass and we don't need to worry about it. My dad's confidence in me was a real booster and made me determined not to let him down. I passed first time.

Can you see that it can make a difference?

FINAL SUMMARY

I hope you have enjoyed reading my book and have learnt that the key 10 minute per day principle can be very effective. On top of this, I hope you have discovered the secrets to why some children perform better at school then others. Remember these were my ways of working and my opinions and they work for me. Whatever you have learnt and however you choose to adopt my tips in your lifestyle, I am sure it will make a difference and make your child stand above their peers.   Some of my tips may not work for everyone, so adopt the ones that do. For those tips you may already be doing, I hope that I have given you confidence to formalise these ways of working to provide maximum impact. Mix and match tips for variety. The key point is to keep up the momentum, stick to your child's goals and watch them achieve.

I hope you can also see, that it is not a big lifestyle change to incorporate some of your time to help you children get ahead in school. They have not missed out on a happy creative childhood, nor have you missed out on your daily life.

Read the 10 minute a day principle again and check out a summary of all the tips in the Index. It will be a useful reminder to help you, help your child. Remember if you miss one session, don't feel guilty because every new day is a fresh day and it brings a new opportunity.

MY GRATITUDE

I want to thank the following books and people who have inspired me to write this book and also made me realise that I CAN do this.

1. Rich Dad Poor Dad book by author Robert Kiyosaki. This book is not written well at all. He openly admits this in his book that he is not a writer, but he had one key message to deliver in the book and that he does. If he could write a book and be super successful – SO CAN I!

2. The Tiger Mother book by author Amy Chua. For making me realise it's not just me that want their children to do well. She also proved that parents need to support their children and help them achieve what they need to. The key thing I learnt here is that "I ain't no tiger mother!" However I can make a difference in my child's life by supporting them to achieve their success.

3. Jesse Brisendine is a life coach and his purpose in life is to empower people to live their lives. I read his inspiring comments on social media everyday and he reminds me to feel empowered and make a change every day. Check out his Jess Brisendine's 1 year 1000 Challenge on Facebook

https://www.facebook.com/1Year1000Challenge
www.jessebrisendine.com

4. My children Mia and Vinnie who put up with my 10 minutes a day investment on most days.

5. The actor Paul Walker for teaching me the phrase Go big or Go home. Paul Walker set up the charity ROWW. Reach out Worldwide was born out of the earthquake that hit Haiti and the charity now helps out when other natural disasters strike. In his own way he has taught me that humanity should be people's first religion. We should help people in any way we can no matter how successful or how busy we are and we must share the love.

WWW.ROWW.ORG

6. My husband for taking the time out and supporting me write this book. He reviewed this book countless times, and without his help, this book would not be as robust as it is.

Finally I want to thank you - my readers - for taking the time to read my book. I hope together we can all make a difference and make the world a better place through education.

Join me and social media, view my tweets and share your thoughts.

FACEBOOK: RI HANNA MISTRY – GET YOUR KIDS AHEAD IN 10 MINUTES PER DAY

HTTPS://WWW.FACEBOOK.COM/GETYOURKIDSAHEAD

TWITTER: #GETYOURKIDSAHEAD
@RIHANNAMISTRY1

HTTPS://TWITTER.COM/RIHANNAMISTRY1

INDEX OF TIPS

Printed in Great Britain
by Amazon